Tales from the Blue

Adventures in Law Enforcement

for Jack

J.B. King

J. B. King

All the events and people discussed in this book are true. Where names are used the individuals were either convicted of a crime, deceased, or agreed for their name to appear in this book.

DEDICATION

This book is dedicated to my son Taylor James King who at a very early age, many years ago, told me I needed to write a book about my Highway Patrol career.

Books by J.B. King:
Justice
The Tilly Treasure
Tales from the Blue: Adventures in Law Enforcement

Upcoming:
A Serial Killer in the Ozarks?
Manhunt: John David Brown

CHAPTER CONTENTS

ACKNOWLEDGMENTS

As the Author I would like to acknowledge and thank Mr. Danny Fry for his help with this book and the use of his special cartoon. That one set the stage for several other cartoons we dreamed up to go with some of the stories in this book. And a special acknowledgement to Natalie Sanders and her Buds at Next Chapter Marking. As the very first customer of the new company we entered into unknown territory together. I can now tell you that they did an outstanding job with the production of this book. If you need help they can provide that help.

FOREWARD

Met J.B. King when he was the sheriff of Pulaski County and I was just starting out as a reporter for the Waynesville Daily Guide. To say he's always been my favorite Pulaski County character would be an understatement.

Through my years at the paper, he finished his last term as sheriff and I went on to become the managing editor of the paper. We built quite the friendship during that time.

While he was researching the Johnny Lee Thornton book in our newspaper archives, we spent a lot of time sitting around trading stories. I've always enjoyed J.B. as a story teller. He reminds me of an uncle sitting on the porch and telling stories about all kinds of fascinating things. In this case, the fascinating thing is the wilder days of Pulaski County.

Boy was it ever wild! We had whore houses, organized crime, drug trafficking, weird, just plain weird, crime, and a very unique variety of crime from the 70's through the 80's. It still has some oddities, but it's nothing like it was then and is actually a wonderful place to raise a family now, but back to J.B.'s stories.

Those visits to our archive and our long discussions about his experiences prompted me to beg, whine, push, and generally poke at him to write a column for the paper. He'd already written two books, but nothing like what I wanted from him and he eventually caved and let me have a Facebook post he'd written about an experience to help me on a rare slow news day.

The column took off. Everyone loved it and his wonderful wife agreed with me about writing the column. The story, which is actually included in this book, with a longer explanation, was about truckers helping him catch a bad guy on the interstate.

The chapters are of varying length because this book is a collection of stories, mostly from his days in the Highway Patrol, when Pulaski County was at its wildest. J.B. has lots of stories and I've really enjoyed working with him over the years, but especially now because I had the honor of being the editor of this book.

We've had fun creating it and I've laughed out loud at the email replies he's sent me in response to questions I had about some of the stories. He's a great story teller, but he was also a great cop. I've known many, many, many cops throughout my years as a journalist and J.B. is by far my favorite.

I actually owe J.B. a debt of gratitude. He's fun, funny, sweet as pie, honorable, but absolutely fearless. He doesn't see himself that way, but because of him and the idea for this book, I finally had the courage to chase my dream. Thank you so much, my friend! Much love.

Natalie Sanders

AUTHOR'S INTRODUCTION

As the author of this book, I would like to welcome you into the wild, wild, world of law enforcement tales from the wilder days of Pulaski County, Missouri. Every story you read in this book is true. Due to the passage of time, I may not remember every detail exactly correct, but the stories have not been embellished. I spent my entire thirty-two year career with the Missouri State Highway Patrol assigned to the Pulaski County Zone of Troop I. I arrived here in December 1969 as the greenest, rawest rookie on the street and when I retired in June 2001 I was the zone commander. I also kept my hand in and served two terms as the Sheriff of Pulaski County, and still serve as a reserve deputy today.

However, this book is not so much about me, repeat, not so much about me, as it is about the mystique of working in the Pulaski County of the 70's and 80's. Other Troopers who worked in Pulaski County for a long period of time have just as many stories as I do about Pulaski County, maybe even more stories. But they are not writing this book, I am, and hence I am in the middle of most of these stories. The big problem with writing this book turned out to be remembering the incidents that had occurred. Once recalled, the incidents were easy to write down and only a few needed additional research.

How do you explain Pulaski County of the 70's to people who did not live here back then? Well, you would start by telling them that in 1939, with World War II on the brink of a shooting war, the United States Army bought close to 80,000 acres of land in Pulaski County to establish the new basic training United States Army base of Fort Leonard Wood. Pulaski County was forever changed after that. What was once a very rural county with a low population total, changed overnight.

The city of Waynesville had approximately 600 residents at the time the establishment of Fort Leonard Wood was announced and within one week the population of Waynesville jumped to 1800 people. The federal government poured millions upon millions of dollars into Ft. Leonard Wood for construction, salaries, and equipment. With the large sums of money suddenly sweeping into the county there came an influx of bad guys who wished to separate the good citizens of the county from their newfound wealth with a multitude of criminal schemes.

Then to make matters worse, the Mother Road, Route 66, and nowadays Interstate 44 runs squarely through the center of the county. This major East-West traffic artery brings in millions more people each year passing through the county. And they frequently stop here. When you have millions of people visiting or passing through each year, there's going to be a certain criminal element that occurs naturally.

The situation in Pulaski County, when I began my first work shift here on January 1, 1970, was very unusual to say the least. The Missouri State Highway Patrol Training Academy had not prepared me for Pulaski County. The Highway Patrol is just that, a Highway Patrol. Our Troopers travel the highways looking for violations of the motor vehicle code and investigate motor vehicle accidents. In a nutshell, traffic enforcement and safety is the name of our game. Once in a while we get into a criminal case. At least that's what members of the Patrol did in every county of the state, except Pulaski County. In Pulaski County, we worked long hours and handled everything you could think of, and some you probably couldn't, of a criminal nature. All crimes of any nature, any time, day or night.

Every police agency in the county was short-staffed, often times with officers who had not been adequately trained, and so virtually every shift you worked you heard somebody on the radio saying we need assistance from the state. And as such, we got into everything. As an example, in 1970, I had 48 criminal arrests and not a single speed device (radar) arrest. I recovered 14 stolen cars that year. I also worked 172 motor vehicle accidents in 1970. I did not get off my Field Training Officer phase, where I rode with a senior Trooper and started solo patrol work until April of 1970. My first year was very busy.

At the time I started working in Pulaski County, we had approximately ten houses of ill repute that were running wide open without hindrance from local law enforcement, a situation State Troopers could do nothing about. As Troopers, we were handicapped by an antique state law which prevented us from making arrests on private property, except in felony situations. The pimps and the ladies of the evening were well aware of that little fact and what they were doing, weren't felonies. And usually they had the good sense not to mess with us. Thankfully that law has now been repealed.

It became a routine operation for us on the night shift, for the two or three Troopers who were working to get together, and we would pick a house of ill repute from the hat. We would then drop by for a visit. Long and bitter experience had taught the local Troopers who worked here, long before I arrived in the county, that it paid to know who was in town and what car they were driving.

Because very frequently, before the night was over in our mix of assaults, robberies, shootings, knifings, and thefts, we were probably going to be looking for one of the cars we had just observed in the parking lot of that particular house of ill repute.

Needless to say, visiting a house of ill repute every work night was not exactly what I thought I had signed up for when I became a Trooper. My wife, and the wives of the other troopers, were really pleased to know that we were on a first name basis with 100 or more prostitutes on any given day of the year. And if you believe that statement I own a bridge that's for sale in New York City. Cheap!

When you add the fact, that in 1970, the Vietnam War was still going hot and heavy and there was a lot of public dissension about the war, we found ourselves in the middle of the great AWOL (Absent With Out Leave) military chase. Young lads, who had been drafted into the Army and discovered that they really did not like the Army, made the unwise decision to walk away on their own, without permission, virtually every day of the year. Frequently, these young lads would take somebody's car, without permission, to make the trip back home easier or they would break into a house because they were cold and hungry and needed more clothing or food. In general, by 1970, the AWOL traffic had reached the point where they really were not welcome in Pulaski County and thus we spent a considerable amount of time chasing AWOL soldiers, as part of our routine day's work.

Another contributing factor to the craziness of Pulaski County during that era, was the so-called "pimp war," a period of time in the late 1960's to early 1970's when rival factions from organized crime groups from the St. Louis, Missouri, area fought with other organized crime members from the Memphis, Tennessee, area for control of the prostitution, drugs, and other illegal practices here in Pulaski County. People were shot and killed routinely, explosives blew up houses, and to say that the county was exciting qualifies as the definite understatement of the year. I believe we had the only Army base in the nation to have a resident FBI office on post, mainly because of the organized crime issues.

So when you put the entire package together, Pulaski County was an exciting and very unusual place where the action went on twenty-four hours a day, seven days a week, and 365 days a year without stop. I think there were several Troopers that I know, myself included, who became addicted to the nonstop action. There will probably be a story or two in this book where the reader will ask themselves, is he kidding? Did that really happen? No I am not and yes it did.

Now, before everybody gets carried away by the doom and gloom words you just read, please understand that the Pulaski County of today (2018) is nothing like the days of old. Our schools are top notch, housing areas have boomed, and we have about 52,000 people currently living in the county. We have a Tourism Bureau that brings in many peaceful people via I-44 to visit. Ft. Wood is now a closed access military base and you need to jump through a hoop or two in order to enter the base. We no longer have pimps, ladies of the evening and houses of ill repute dotting our landscape. They all disappeared many years ago thanks to the efforts of law enforcement, city councils, and the cooperation of all involved. We are now a typical Midwest county with some crime and a serious drug problem, like everybody else, along with a heavy traffic flow. But the total crime scene now is far different than it was in the 1970's. And for that I am quite happy.

And so, today, you now have a chance to explore the mystique of working in the Pulaski County of that time. This book has quite a few stories about events that occurred in Pulaski County during the 1970's, 1980's, and maybe even a story or two from the 1990's. Enjoy!

J. B. King, MSHP 733

1 ROOKIE DAY ONE, THE FIRST WORK SHIFT

And on this date in history, 48 years ago, Jan. 1, 1970, a very nervous young and very green new Trooper was picked up at his residence for his first ever official workday by his field training officer (FTO) just before 4 p.m. and we were off to the wild, wild, west night shift of Pulaski County. The FTO's stern words of wisdom were, "Stick to me like my shadow."

My response was, "Yes sir." And that worked out well until just after 7 p.m., when we arrived at a disturbance involving about ten men and two firearms at a business in the county.

My FTO was swarmed under by about six guys, several with bloody heads, who all ignored the green Trooper and went to the experienced man. While FTO was trying to get the story, one other guy approached me and told me a guy with a gun was holding his buddies inside the building and several of them were hurt.

Goodbye FTO, see you later, as I went into the building and disarmed the bad guy at gunpoint. I have no clue why I did this, but in this case the bad guy with the gun inside the building turned out to be the owner of the business. He was defending his property and immediately laid down the weapon when ordered to do so.

My thoughts at the time were, "But wait a second three hours into my first shift and guns! I signed up for this job? What was I thinking? Was I thinking?"

And thus began my education into the results of mixing beer, temper, and firearms together in one scene. Usually a very bad decision.

Much later, after we got the situation under total control and took our enforcement action, the FTO and I had a little talk. During "the talk," after a long period of time in which he spoke and I was quiet, he finally conceded that well actually, that duh, ugh, oops, oh damn, I had acted properly under the circumstances and modified his words of wisdom to, "Stay as close to me as my shadow whenever possible."

At the time, I did not understand the pressure the FTO was under being held responsible for the new nugget rookie Trooper, that he really did not know yet or know how said rookie would react in a dangerous situation. A definite strain on the emotions, as I found out many years later, when I became the FTO and went out for that first ever shift with my new nugget rookie Trooper.

In the aftermath of this first working shift ever in Pulaski County, I found myself remembering something that my father had told me. When he first learned that I had been assigned to Pulaski County, he said to me, "You know why you're being sent there don't you?"

I said, "Yes it's an assignment."

Dad said, "No, it's because you are single. That means your expendable." Gee thanks dad, but after the first shift I kind of wondered if father was always right.

2 THE HOUSE MOVER

Pulaski County always provided some of the oddest ticket writing a trooper could ever write and some seriously strange situations. I don't think there are many other officers out there that can say they responded to a traffic accident involving a house in the middle of the road.

Way back in the 1970's, the very early 1970's, there used to be an enterprising businessman in the community who made a pretty penny through the purchase of large buildings on Fort Leonard Wood that had been declared surplus. Once purchased he would then move the house to a location where the new homeowners eagerly awaited.

The only problem was these houses were so large you could not get an over dimension permit from the state of Missouri to legally move the houses. As a result, these house moves were usually made very late Saturday night, early Sunday morning, with very few people knowing what was happening.

However, on this particular occasion, I got called out of bed at 5 o'clock in the morning to go to what is now known as VFW Road just 200 or 300 yards west of where it joins the small circular drive there in St. Robert, by the Hub Restaurant. There was a reported motor vehicle accident situation involving lines down, both power lines and telephone lines.

Upon arrival on the scene, I find myself looking at a house blocking the road completely. A quick investigation revealed that the man on the roof, with the broom, who was supposed to be lifting the power lines and telephone lines up with the broom over the high point of the house and then walking the length of the house, as it passed under the lines, and then dropping the lines safely back down behind the house, had completely failed in his job. If I remember correctly, not only were several lines down, I believe one electric pole had been broken off.

Instant analysis of the situation: we have a mess, a really big mess. And then even more craziness.

Suddenly, I hear screams, and a screaming lady comes charging down the gravel road from the spur, with her pimp in hot pursuit waving a metal dog chain. I quickly stepped out from behind the house blocking the roadway into their path. The lady disappeared completely because I was watching the pimp with the metal chain. However, the situation diffused rather rapidly when the pimp saw that my hand was grasping the handgrip on my revolver and I was ready to draw. The pimp threw down the chain and ran back to the establishment.

When I got to the establishment, he had disappeared and I contacted the other half of the pimp team that ran the place and asked for an explanation. The explanation was the girl had not distributed her profits from the evening before correctly and the pimp, also the husband half of the ownership team, was a little bit drunk and got a little carried away. Since I could not identify the lady of the evening who was being pursued and no blows had been struck, I realized it was a useless endeavor to continue and the other half of the pimp team assured me that she would corral her husband immediately. In her case, her word had usually been good in the past and so I trusted that it would be good again. I returned to my house.

I might be slightly off on some of the figures because this happened a long time ago, but the house that was blocking the road was approximately 85 or 90 feet long, 26 feet wide and almost 21 feet tall. Major, major, violations of the over dimension laws currently in effect in the state of Missouri. But now that you have the house "caught" what are you going to do with it?

By this time, several other Troopers had come on the air expecting a peaceful Sunday morning shift and they were now out there with me at the scene of this mess. We put our heads together and we could not think of a place, public or private, where we could park a house this size, knowing full well that it could not be legally moved again under any circumstance. Wherever we left this monster, there it would stay.

The only practical decision was for us to become house movers and assist in the delivery of the house to a location on Mo. 17 about two miles west of Rt. T. The new home owner was waiting for the house and had a spot cleared for the package. Unbelievably, I was now doing duty as a house mover in an illegal house move!

So for the next three hours or so, we blocked traffic and detoured early Sunday morning drivers around the monster home, as it slowly moved down the roads. This time the guy on the roof used his broom correctly.

Once the home was delivered, I sat the illegal house mover down and issued him ten uniform traffic tickets for the house move and for the aggravation, I added one extra for the expired plates on one of his trucks.

I was not present when he went to court and pled guilty. But I was later told that he griped to the Judge about the excessive ticket toll, because costs like that would put him out of business. My informant said the Judge was not impressed. Case Closed.

3 HOW UNDERWEAR AND A DRUNK SAVED A LIFE

We have always been blessed, or maybe I should say cursed, here in Pulaski County by the presence of some very enthusiastic and hardworking Conservation Agents. While they usually object to us referring to them as the "Skunk Sheriff" they have always worked well with us "taillight detectives." And somehow, whenever I was around them, things always seemed to go downhill..

The case in question was on a hot summer night. The game wardens had been having problems with drunks at the Riddle Bridge Fishing Access Point for several weeks and, on this night, they vowed to do some heavy enforcement action on the access. About 10:00 p.m. that night, the Pulaski County Sheriff's Dispatch radioed our game agent that drunks were alleged to be shooting up the access site. The agent advised that he was enroute and he was warned there were supposed to be a bunch of them.

So little old me and another Trooper decided to head

that way for backup if it was needed and we also suspected the game warden's arrival on the scene would probably persuade some drunks to drive away from the access point. Easy picking for a DWI charge. But our plan failed.

None of us were even close to the fishing access when the sheriff's dispatch told the game agent that the biggest problem children had left in a green El Camino pickup a few minutes prior. Just seconds later, our agent radioed back to us that he had just been run off the road by said green El Camino. I tried to get to a road intersection where I could park and wait for them, but instead I met them on a hillcrest and I got run off the road. I radioed a warning back to the other Trooper.

I was able to get back on the road and start after them. One minute later, I saw the other Trooper in the distance and there were no cars between us. The only place the pickup could have gone was a county road off to the right. I took that road and immediately saw dust and, about thirty seconds later, I saw a red taillight in the distance. I was able to quickly catch up to the vehicle and it was our bad guy.

Being drunk, he could not stop on the long straight stretch of road with great visibility. He had to wait until he rounded a very sharp and blind curve before stopping. The big danger now was other officers crashing into us as they tried to catch up to the mini-chase.

I had my bright vehicle mounted spotlight aimed at the truck. In the truck bed, in a lawn chair facing toward the rear of the truck, was a drunk male. He paid no attention to me as I walked up to the truck cab. Not only did he pay no attention to me, it appeared he did not know I was there or that my spotlight was in his face.

Can you say totally hammered barely able to remain upright? How did he stay in the bed of the truck during the chase? And even better at the conclusion of the action on this stop, he was still seated there, totally oblivious to his surroundings or the events of the past few minutes.

The vehicle driver was also fairly well hammered and I ordered him out of the vehicle to begin the DWI field testing. As I did that, I took note of his front seat passenger, Joe Cool, who had no shoes or socks, no shirt, and was wearing only cut off blue jeans. He had his hands clasped together over his stomach and was ignoring me completely. However, he did appear to be awake and halfway alert.

As I began to examine and question the driver, my fellow Trooper came up and got his driver's license and went back to his patrol car to run the driver for prior DWI's. Right after my Trooper backup got to his car, I saw Joe Cool reach for the handle on the passenger door. He twisted his body sideways and used his left arm to reach across his body and grab the door handle. Very odd move. I continued to watch him as he got out of the truck. He then suddenly turned back toward me and he was drawing a pistol from his waistband.

Red Alert!!

I was facing deadly danger, he was already drawing his gun before I even saw the threat and to make matters worse, I was standing at the driver's side door and he the passenger door. One very small bench seat in a truck was between us. Point blank range! A shot would not miss.

He was also drunk and the front sight on his pistol evidently caught in his underwear and he was having trouble drawing the gun out. I beat him to the draw and he was looking down the barrel of my .357 revolver.

He was not impressed and continued to tug at his weapon. Meanwhile I started shouting useless commands such as, "Stop", "Don't move" and so forth. He still was not impressed and continued to tug at the gun.

After what seemed like a few hours, as he tugged on the gun, it came clear and he moved it into a position where it was pointed my way, but then he moved it to a 45 degree angle slightly away from me. I fully recognized that a simple flick of his wrist and the gun would be pointed directly at me.

I continued with the useless commands, "Drop the gun!" "Don't move", repeat as needed.

It was needed, but the little voice in the back of my head was screaming, "You don't need to shoot him!"

After another hour or so, well, probably more like a few seconds, he laid the gun down on the seat, but kept his hand hovering directly over it as in that famous western movie scene with the gun on the bar in the saloon. Draw pilgrim!

I gave more useless commands, "Don't touch the gun!" "Step away from the gun!"

He was not impressed.

While this six hour ordeal was going on, Okay, it was probably not much more than 30-40 seconds tops, but it sure as hell felt like six hours. Meanwhile my backup was happily chatting away on the radio just twenty yards away from me. He might as well have been on the reverse side of the Moon. Our stalemate continued. The drunk with the gun was still not impressed with me.

And then decisive action! The drunk driver finally understood that friend Joe was about to get his head blown off and the drunk driver began to stumble away from me. He weaved and stumbled around the front end of the truck and wobbled up to Joe. He then violently shoved Joe backwards, down over an embankment, and saved the day. The pistol was left on the front seat by the sudden departure of Joe Cool. My backup saw the shove and charged up ready for combat.

Thanks partner could not have done this one without you.

And so, in conclusion, nobody got hurt during this incident and the drunk driver of this truck became the first drunk driver I ever apologized to for having had to arrest him for DWI. But I did just happen to mention his good deed to the Judge.

As my backup Trooper loaded Joe Cool into his vehicle, for a trip to the jail, I found myself standing there holding his weapon thinking that it would make a great handgun for squirrel hunting. I really began to admire the weapon the longer I held the gun. I knew that in the near future I would have to buy one. I did.

Later that night as I reviewed my actions in this case my question was, "Am I normal anymore? The guy may have tried to shoot me with the pistol and my reaction was to spend several minutes admiring the gun?"

4 ILLINOIS, DID YOU HATE ME?

As before mentioned, stolen cars seemed to be a good part of the job in Pulaski County back in the day, but there was a period of time where they were particularly prevalent. The next chapters are dedicated to some very interesting stolen car incidents.

I think the folks living in Illinois had it in for me in the 1970's. It seemed that I constantly ran into vehicles from that great state that had been borrowed or taken by force from their rightful owners and then driven across my path. So here are three such stories of stolen cars from the land of Lincoln.

During the summer of 1970 I was on the city route in St. Robert, Missouri, one day when a local business owner flagged me down and complained about some "hippies" in a big Buick car that had damaged a sign on the parking lot of his business. So I followed him back to his business and there I found two 1970's era hippies with the stereotypical tie-dyed T-shirts and long hair. They were standing next to a Buick 225 sedan with Illinois plates.

The property owner got into my patrol car with me and

we discussed the situation. He was not too happy to find out, that as a member of the patrol, I could not arrest them on private property for having damaged his sign. However, I did place a radio call into the St. Robert Police and asked them to send a unit to the scene.

While this was going on, the female member of the hippie tribe made two trips to the little girl's room and then back to the vehicle. The male member of the hippie tribe simply watched me, and the way he stared at me started my little alarm bell ringing. I gave the vehicle plate to Troop I for a registration and stolen check, but in those days the process was a lot more cumbersome and it took a while to receive answers.

When I got an answer back from Troop I on the license plate, the situation took a decided nosedive for the worse. Just as Troop I started to tell me that the vehicle had been reported stolen, the two people jumped in the vehicle and peeled out of the parking lot.

The chase was on, a phrase you may read a lot in this book.

The stolen vehicle turned right and headed toward Waynesville. As we went down the long hill into Waynesville, which at the time was a two lane road, the driver of the Buick passed several cars on the hill right into the face of oncoming traffic. I had to dodge that traffic, and as such, by the time I got to the bottom of the hill, I had lost sight of the vehicle.

There were a number of pedestrians walking around the courthouse in Waynesville, on the Square, and none of them seemed to be excited about a high-speed car driving past the courthouse, so I immediately made a right turn onto Highway 17 and started toward Crocker, Missouri. Within just a few hundred yards, I caught sight of the car again about a quarter mile ahead of me. And about the time I saw the car, the driver lost control, went off the left side of the road and overturned down the embankment.

I braked to a halt on Mo. 17 just above them and ran

down over the hill to confront my car thieves. I removed the driver from the car at shotgun point. I marched him back to the trunk of the car and had him spread eagle over the trunk. The female passenger was getting out of the car on her own and I ran up to the passenger side door to escort her back to the trunk area.

At that point, things went a whole lot more downhill. The female passenger looked at me for a moment and then dived back into the front seat of the car and began frantically searching for something underneath the car seat. I, of course, was shouting, "stop, don't do that," and other such words of wisdom, which she completely ignored.

Not finding what she was looking for under the seat, she moved her search to the glovebox of the car. Again more words of "stop, halt, don't," which are another group of words that I uttered many times in my career. Meanwhile the male passenger, who was wearing a really long oversized shirt, was watching me out of the corner of his eyes. His look made it obvious that he had a weapon and was looking for a chance to use that weapon.

Finally, at last the female found what she wanted. She had gone back underneath the front seat again and then she came whirling around toward me with her right hand extended toward me with something in the hand. Her left hand was moving toward the object for a two-handed grip. I began to squeeze the trigger on my shotgun. At the extreme last microsecond of time I realized that she had a pack of cigarettes in her hand. I relaxed my finger on the trigger and at the time halfway wondered why the gun had not fired. I had pulled the trigger. I then escorted her to the rear of the vehicle and she was spread eagled over the trunk.

We stood that way for several minutes until a backup car finally arrived. Another Trooper, who will not be named, charged down to the scene and immediately started to frisk the female passenger. As his hands closed around the front of her chest, he found a pair of unencumbered size forty or so D cup female body parts.

The look of complete surprise on his face was priceless. Equally priceless was the look of contempt on the face of the female as she turned her head around to glare at him.

Once he finished the frisk of the female, the other Trooper turned his attention to the male and quickly removed an 8 inch butcher knife from his waistband. Both suspects were handcuffed and transported to the Pulaski County Sheriff's office. However, as we had stood there talking to them before they were transported we realized that they were "high" on something. After the suspects had been removed from the scene, I thoroughly searched the car and found nothing.

A short time later we received a call from the owner of the business in St. Robert asking me to return to the scene. When I got there he handed me a plastic bag full of prescription pills that the female had hidden in the toilet at his business.

The prosecuting attorney filed multiple charges for drug possession and possession of a stolen vehicle against the two subjects and they were held in custody until Illinois authorities extradited them back to the state of Illinois on the auto theft charge, at which time, the local charges were dropped. Case closed.

The next Illinois case of note, I ended up writing a speeding ticket for the driver for driving five miles over the limit. Not a standard practice.

It was a fine evening shift and things were jumping. Troop I radio put out a BOLO (Be On The Lookout) for a described vehicle with Illinois license plates that had just left a gas station at the Missouri Highway 28 overpass without paying for eighteen or twenty dollars' worth of gasoline. I was in an excellent position and a few minutes later I found myself behind the vehicle in question pacing along with him as he drove west.

The car maintained a steady 60 miles an hour in a 55

mile an hour speed limit. Due to a quirk in the Missouri law at the time I could not arrest the man for leaving without paying for gasoline. So I made a vehicle traffic stop for a speed violation.

The subject was friendly and talkative and he readily admitted that he had no money and that's why he left without paying. He even showed me his empty wallet. When I inquired about the vehicle he said that his good buddy Pete had loaned it to him so he could make a trip to Arizona. Unfortunately the registration to the vehicle did not come back to a man named Pete. But there was no stolen report on the vehicle. However by this time the suspect and I had talked long enough that my criminal recognition senses were twitching.

I suspected that the vehicle was actually stolen. So the only course of action I could take was to write him a speed ticket for 5 miles an hour over the limit. The only such low speed ticket I ever wrote in my career. And of course since he was from Illinois, a land of full of people who had ignored Missouri traffic citations and now had active warrants for their arrest, I needed him to post bond. So I transported him to the Pulaski County Sheriff's office to post that bond. And surprise he had no money and was unable to post a bond. He was incarcerated.

I then got on the telephone and began calling numbers in Illinois. Pete or whatever his name was, was not at home. I called the police department in that small Illinois city and filled them in on my suspicion. They promised me they would get right on it and see what they could find out. Approximately three hours later, the police in that small town called back and reported that they had found the registered owner of the vehicle in an adjoining town. In fact he was in the hospital in that adjoining town recovering from the severe beating he had taken when his car was stolen by a suspect who was described and sounded quite a bit like my car driver.

Then the police in the other town where the theft had

actually occurred contacted us and before long a felony warrant was issued in the state of Illinois. Our suspect here waived extradition, and the police from Illinois drove down and picked him up and took him back home. Case closed.

5 OPERATION YELLOW

Illinois continued to have it out for me, but this next case hurt my poor stomach. Once in a while, really weird circumstances would come together and give you a story to tell that nobody would believe.

This particular story started out late at night when a local restaurant owner who was a friend of ours called Sarge, a fellow trooper, and told him that if he could find some bananas she would make us a banana pudding. This particular restaurant owner was noted for her outstanding banana pudding which Sarge and I had both had on several occasions in the past. And since Sarge and I were the only two cars on this night it was quickly obvious that if we could find some bananas we were going to share a great dessert together. And so operation yellow was hatched.

Throughout our working years in Pulaski County, we always had to keep in mind the fact that there were many thousands of police scanners in our area and that every word we said on the radio was going to be known to thousands of people. Knowing this, we frequently rigged up code words for particular situations especially if the topic was sensitive.

And thus for the next hour or so the two way radio traffic between Sarge and I had a lot of references like; "the 28 overpass where that place there only has green, no yellow."

"10-4, how about the place at Buckhorn? I'm headed that way. Okay, no dice here, more green, no yellow."

After several other such conversations took place over the radio, I feel fairly certain that a lot of people were wondering just what in the hell was going on.

And then disaster struck.

I was out in the west end of Pulaski County, heading for another possible yellow location, when I saw a vehicle with Illinois plates parked on the road shoulder. As I parked behind the vehicle, I saw man about 20 yards in front of the vehicle walking away from the vehicle. I quickly made contact with the man and asked him if his car had broken down. He gave me a rather forceful and emphatic answer that it was not his car and he knew nothing about the car.

A much too forceful and much too emphatic answer, it seemed to me. Alarm bells started sounding. As I continued to talk to him, his responses made no sense and he was clearly a person who did not like police officers. After just a moment or two, I did a quick frisk of his person for my safety and pulled a Rohm .22 revolver from his waistband. I then arrested him for carrying a concealed weapon and off to the Pulaski County Jail we went once again.

Once again, I was making a telephone call to the registered owner of the vehicle, who lived in the Village of Maryville, Illinois. And once again, the owner could not be found. The local police department was then contacted for information.

At this time I would like to tell the rest of the story by quoting from a letter that Troop I received from Chief John C. Lucas Jr., of the Village of Maryville Police

Department; *"On June 21, 1979, Trooper King apprehended a person wanted by this department for armed robbery, aggravated battery, and the theft of an automobile. However, at the time, Trooper King was unaware of these charges. But, being a thorough and dedicated police officer, he sensed something wrong with the subject hitchhiking next to a disabled automobile in a ditch. At this time, Trooper King, put two and two together, linked the subject with the disabled auto, and also discovered a concealed weapon upon his person. Trooper King immediately arrested him."*

"The Illinois Secretary of State computer was down when a check of the auto was made by Trooper King, consequently leaving it an unknown fact that the car was stolen. Trooper King pursued the matter further, at which time he came in contact with this department, and was informed that the car was in fact stolen however, for some reason, it was not entered on the computer as stolen."

Having been informed of the arrest by Trooper King, myself and Officer Schneider of this department, took the victim to the Pulaski County Jail, where the victim identified the suspect. On January 3, 1980, through the efforts of the Maryville Police Department and the Missouri Highway Patrol's James B. King, the defendant, Bill Darrell Turner, pled guilty to the armed robbery charge and was sentenced to six years in the penitentiary." Criminal case closed.

As for operation yellow, it turned out that, while I was playing with the Illinois stolen vehicle, Sarge had indeed found yellow gold and had delivered it to our friend. Unfortunately when it came time to pick up the results of operation yellow, I was still busy playing detective and so Sarge was forced to take possession of the 9 x 13" baking pan full of banana pudding all by himself.

When I finally caught up with Sarge and the pan about forty-eight hours later, there was a 2" x 2" square of banana pudding left in one corner of the pan. Operation yellow turned out to be very disappointing for me.

6 THE PIMP BLOOD RELAY

During the decade of the 1970's, one of the more common jobs that we Troopers did was known as the blood relay. The American Red Cross maintained a headquarters in Springfield, Missouri, where whole blood was stocked. Whenever a hospital throughout the Southwest region of Missouri needed whole blood, on a rush basis, the American Red Cross would prepare a box with the blood and ice inside and would call Troop D Headquarters in Springfield to start the relay.

The Troop D officer would pick the blood up and get it started in whatever direction it was going. The box of blood was passed from one Trooper to another, in each of the zones that it went through, and each Trooper hauling the blood for a leg of the journey would run red lights and sirens up until the meeting point with the next Trooper. As a general rule, we got the blood to the hospitals PDQ.

One nice night shift, I was notified of an emergency blood relay coming in headed for the Pulaski County Hospital. I filled up my gas tank and moved out to the Laclede/Pulaski County line to meet the blood relay and upon receiving the blood I started East with the red lights and siren activated.

Upon my arrival at the Pulaski County Hospital, my own personal physician, Dr. Harvey E. Nichols met me at the back door. I handed him the box of blood.

Harvey looked at me with a big grin on his face and said, "Congratulations! You just saved the life of..." and he named one of our most prominent pimps in the area.

Rats!

According to Harvey, the pimp told him that he had heard a suspicious noise outside of his residence. When he reached up into his closet to retrieve his forty-five caliber pistol, from the shelf up high, it had somehow fallen to the ground and discharged in the process, striking him squarely in the chest. However, the chest wound was on a horizontal level through and through, not a vertical up and down wound. The pimp needed a better story to explain the wound. But still, our pimp was in bad shape and the blood I had just brought to the hospital was most likely going to save the day.

The blood relay did save the day. In the years that followed, every time I had to deal with said pimp, I reminded him that one day I had helped to save his life and that he should be very nice to me and give me no trouble.

 He never did.

Postscript: I have an urge to pay tribute to a member of the greatest American generation who is no longer with us. Dr. Harvey E. Nichols, a man who used his World War II G.I. Bill benefits to attend medical school in Kirksville, Missouri, and who eventually ended up in Waynesville as a doctor. One fine day, while visiting with him as a patient, I mentioned his World War II days as a tail gunner on a B-25 bomber during combat missions over Italy. I had been researching past newspaper files for an article I was going to do on the World War II veterans in our community and was fishing for more information.

The next thing I know, Doc had his arms sweeping all

around the office as he described the pursuit curves and the strafing runs made by the German Messerschmitt Bf 109's and the Focke-Wulf 190 fighter aircraft attacking his bomber. He then proceeded to describe how you had to compute the lead angle to return fire at them with the twin fifty caliber Browning machine guns in the tail gun position on the B-25.

We had a rather engrossing fifteen minute or so World War II fight going that was quite interesting. Unfortunately, his senior nurse finally came in and basically said, "Uh, Doc, knockoff play time. You have patients waiting." The World War II session ended and Doc went back to work. Harvey was a real good man, may he rest in peace.

.

7 THE SNIPER AND THE COW

The night shifts in Pulaski County were usually the most exciting and had the most cases where high adventure occurred during your work shift. One fine summer night, during the early 1970's, we were notified by the Pulaski County Sheriff's Department that several local youths, in the Buckhorn area, had surprised some men in a farmer's field who had shot and killed cattle.

If I remember correctly, one or two cows had been shot and killed and the subjects were attempting to butcher them when the youths chased them off. The young men were able to advise that there were two white male suspects and they gave a good description of the suspect vehicle.

There were only two Troopers working this night, so my partner and I put our heads together and for some reason we were both positive that these guys were going to try this again. The two of us headed for different sections of county and we began driving county roads, looking for the vehicle in question. I had been just north of Waynesville and had finished running a couple roads out and was driving through town heading toward the Rt. H area.

As I drove through town, I was talking on my CB radio, channel 3, which was used by a lot of local people. I was talking to the late Wendell Wilson when, suddenly, Wendell broke off and began talking to somebody else that I could not hear. A moment later, Wendell told me that George Barry, a farmer that I knew well and who is also now deceased, had just discovered people in his back pasture and he had cows down. George was now chasing the suspect vehicle on the county road toward the end of Route H.

A moment or so later, Wendell relayed the information to me from George that the suspects had put their car in the ditch. He said that, when he approached the suspects, they pulled a rifle on him. George wisely retreated. George gave us the location of the disabled car in the ditch.

Running code 3 to the scene, with full emergency light bar and siren turned on, I was soon parked behind the suspect vehicle. As I got out of my patrol car, I took about two steps toward the disabled vehicle, when the hair on the back of my neck went straight up just like a dog's.

This phenomenon had never happened to me before and I suddenly found myself crouching down in the roadside ditch. The hair on the back of my neck continued to be standing straight up and I stayed in the ditch. It was a dark still night and I could not see anything. The only thing I could hear was the engine on my patrol car and the mechanical turning of the red lights in my emergency light bar.

Frankly I felt like an idiot, but I stayed in the ditch. Due to the traffic on the police channel radios and the CB radios, we soon had a small crowd of people on the scene with six or seven people walking around the cars. I finally convinced myself to get up out of the ditch and join them. At this point, we had no clue which way to start looking for the bad guys that we knew had to be on foot nearby, but we were surrounded by 360° of forest and pasture with no clue as to where to start.

And then the situation changed.

We saw two white males walking up the hill toward us on Route H. As they got closer, the older subject said, "We are the guys you're looking for."

We swarmed all around these two individuals. They were one older male in his 30's and one younger male in his middle teens. George immediately identified the older subject as the driver of the vehicle and the guy who pointed the rifle at him. It was quite obvious that the driver was intoxicated so my fellow trooper made a DWI arrest on the spot and took him to the zone office for a breathalyzer test.

I stayed on the scene with the young juvenile and began to question him about the cattle killings, as well as the location of the missing rifle. After a few minutes, the kid finally told us that the rifle was on the hillside about 80 yards away behind a fallen down log. The young kid took us there and when we got to the log we found that the rifle was balanced on top of the log pointed directly at my patrol car.

After a minute or two, the young lad confessed that, when the first officer arrived on the scene, his uncle was trying to get a shot at the officer with the rifle, but the guy kept ducking down into the ditch and uncle could not get a shot off at him. I took the rifle in hand and sighted toward my vehicle.

I realized that I had been a sitting duck and the only thing that might have saved me was the drunk rifleman might have missed with his trusty .22 rifle. This was a very cold and chilling moment to ponder.

I seized the rifle and we took the young lad and the rifle back to town where we turned the kid over to the Pulaski County Juvenile Officer. I kept the rifle for evidence. By this time, the Pulaski County Sheriff's Department was in a position to exchange information with us and we compared notes on the crimes. During this process, we figured out that, in between shooting two different bunches of cows, our suspects had visited a trailer in the Buckhorn area. We decided to visit that trailer.

It turned out that the trailer in question was owned by the brother of our main suspect. While we were standing in the kitchen telling him that his brother and his nephew were in custody for cattle rustling, we inquired if he had any knowledge of cattle rustling and or the butchering of beef. The owner of the trailer had several questions and he seemed to have difficulty understanding what kind of beef we were talking about. The Deputy Sheriff who was with us was very patiently explaining to him the fact that the brother and nephew had killed several cows and had used a hacksaw to cut the hindquarters off of the cattle.

While this discussion was in progress I looked around the kitchen and I noticed a big beef roast section that had been cooked resting on a platter on the kitchen countertop. The end bone of the beef roast was showing and it had a crinkle cut edge on it sort of like a wavy potato chip, which looked exactly like the end of the bone on the hindquarters of the cow that had been in the trunk of the suspect vehicle.

When the owner of the trailer asked the deputy again, "What kind of beef are you talking about?" I answered his question. As I slowly moved my finger over the end of the bone in the beef roast I told him we were looking for beef with a cut about like this.

His response was more or less, "Oh that kind of beef. There's about 50 pounds of it in the freezer."

The Pulaski County Deputy immediately took over and seized the beef from the refrigerator and made arrangements for the owner of the trailer to have a visit with the judge on a misdemeanor receiving stolen property charge. Case closed.

Postscript: although I faced people in Pulaski County

many times with guns pointed at me. And many times I had been in a dark scary position with people nearby that I suspected were armed and did not like police officers, the hair on the back of my neck had never stood up before this date. And I might add that it has never done so since. But rest assured if you are ever with me on the scene of some breaking situation and the hair on the back of my neck stands straight up like a dogs again, you will find me down low in the nearest ditch. I have no explanation for why the standing hair occurred during this event and this event only.

To follow-up on this case, the following was the outcome. The youths had found one 800 pound cow and two calves, one 500 pound and one 400 pound that had been killed. The cattle carried the 44 brand which was registered to Storie Farms, owned and operated by Emerson and Charlie Storie of Waynesville.

In March of 1976 the three young men; Mike Hendrix, David Hendrix, and Randy Ellzey were presented with as $500.00 check from the Pulaski County Farm Bureau Association for their part in helping to apprehend and convict the cattle rustler. Robert Watts was convicted of stealing cattle in Pulaski County Circuit Court on December 17, 1975, and was sentenced to eight years in the Missouri State Penitentiary system.

8 THE FISHING VIOLATION

There are many things in this world that will get a police officer into trouble. Women and booze are at the top of the list, but boredom and the desire to play a prank on an unsuspecting person have also snagged their share of officers. On this particular unknown date in history during the summer of 1982 my desire to play a prank on a friend got the best of me..

I found myself at the Riddle Bridge fishing access on Route Y one bright sunny summer day. This fishing access was maintained by the Missouri Department of Conservation and features a very nice concrete ramp that backs right down into the Gasconade River to assist fishermen in loading and unloading their boats into the river.

At least that's the official reason why the concrete ramp is there. But other folks have been known to back down the ramp to the water's edge and then burn their way up the ramp laying down smoke from the tires on their automobile and in general creating havoc. This particular location has already starred in a story in this book, so you can imagine the kinds of shenanigans that happen there.

Anyone remember Joe Cool from chapter 3? Now to get back on track.

On this particular occasion, it appeared that the kiddies were having fun peeling out on the ramp, and things were going good, until the young lad in the Volkswagen Beetle accidentally placed his manual shift transmission into reverse and peeled out backwards on the ramp at the water's edge. The Beetle Bug entered the water with a fair amount of speed and floated about 40 yards out into the middle of the stream and was then carried downstream just a few feet before the water entering the vehicle accomplished the unfortunate effect of sinking the good ship Beetle Bug to the bottom of the Gasconade River.

At that point, I was summoned to the scene to prepare an official accident report covering this unfortunate incident. The owner of the vehicle reached the conclusion that he really did want his favorite Beetle Bug back and he engaged the services of one Danny Fry, professional wrecker driver from Poor Boy's Auto Salvage, to retrieve his unfortunate vehicle from the bottom of the river.

My good friend Danny was up to the task and soon had a few hundred feet of steel wrecker cable, with a big hook on the end in his hand, and was diving repeatedly to the bottom of the river. After quite a few attempts, an extremely wet wrecker driver finally managed to get a hook attached underneath the vehicle and was able to pull the poor soaked Beetle Bug from the river.

During this lengthy period of time, while Danny was trying to fish the poor car out of the river, I had been standing around with basically nothing to do and was getting bored. That's when the desire to prank my friend Danny struck me right between the eyes.

I quickly dreamed up a fiendish plot.

I grabbed my official Missouri State Highway Patrol Uniform Traffic Citation book and filled out an official Uniform Traffic Ticket for Mr. Fry charging him with the violation of fishing without a license. It was a well done citation. I even had the correct Missouri statute for fishing without a license listed on the ticket.

Upon presenting said ticket to Mr. Fry, he immediately protested the charge. However, I quickly explained to him that he had a line in the river with a hook on it and there was a skinny chunk of meat on the hook in the water so therefore he was fishing. Everybody laughed but Danny.

And so said ticket was funny as could be until about two weeks later, when I received unexpected high-ranking visitors from troop headquarters. It quickly developed that there had been a most unfortunate, unexpected, never done before, but now was an urgent need, to do a complete audit of every uniform traffic citation in the possession of the Missouri State Highway Patrol. And my little fishing violation charge had come to their attention.

Now at this point I could tell a couple of lies, but the truth of the matter is the ranking gentlemen were not impressed with my little prank, and at the conclusion of their sermon, I vowed that I would never ever do such a despicable thing again. As they drove away, I stood there firmly grasping my posterior portion which had been badly damaged by the sermon. And for the record, these days Danny will laugh wildly about this incident. Especially the "aftermath" part.

Postscript: No, Danny did not have to go to court on my little prank UTT. It was strictly a joke. But when I went to see Danny during the production phase of this book in June of 2018 to obtain a signed release from him in order to name him in this story, I found out for the first time that there was more to this story. It seems that his, at that time, eight year old son Donny thought the whole fishing without a license affair was quite funny. Donny drew a cartoon scene recreating the event as he saw it in his eight year old mind. The framed cartoon has hung on the office wall at Poor Boy Auto Salvage ever since 1982. Solid proof that I will never live this prank down.

Danny Fry's son, Donny, drew a cartoon of the Fishing Violation when he was eight-years-old. This framed drawing has been hanging in the Poor Boy's office ever since.

9 AFTERNOON DELIGHT

A routine working day in Pulaski County could bring just about anything to the front and you could respond to just about any kind of a call you could imagine. And there were quite a few calls you could not imagine. Sometimes these calls require a delicate touch of written prose to explain.

This particular call happened in the very early afternoon hours on a nice clear day. It occurred within the city limits of St. Robert, however, there were no St. Robert officers supposedly available to handle this call. As you read on, you'll understand why I maintain suspicion about whether or not someone could take the call, due to the nature of this one.

Upon my arrival at the scene, I found the following circumstances. It seems that daddy had driven to the local trailer court to take care of some business and when he parked his vehicle, he left it running and did not engage the parking brake. He also parked it on a steep incline and left his thirteen-year-old son in the vehicle. Yes, a recipe for disaster, and disaster occurred when the young lad fiddled around with the controls of the motor vehicle.

The car rolled backwards down a steep grade, crossed over a St. Robert City street, and then smashed into the end of a trailer in the next lower trailer space. Since the car had been in motion, crossing a city street, it qualified as a traffic accident and I was sent to do the written accident report honors.

Arriving on the scene, I quickly discovered that we had two injuries in this accident that were definitely not normal injuries. The explanation concerning the injuries will require a certain amount of delicate wording. When the car crashed into the end of the trailer, it penetrated into a bedroom. And in that bedroom, against the wall that was breached, was a bed. And when the car punched into the bedroom it shoved the bed violently backwards about eight feet. At the time of the accident that bed was occupied by a man and woman engaged in what we shall call afternoon delight. I think somebody wrote a song about that phrase one time.

I entered the bedroom looking for the injured parties and found both the male and female sitting on the edge of the bed. Both were bent over at the waist with their hands holding the frontal genital area on their body. Both were moaning and groaning non-stop. Every so often the male would reach up and rub the top of his head complaining about his head hurting. Try asking silly accident related questions under these circumstances.

Meanwhile, just outside the front door of the damaged trailer, daddy was in the process of killing the thirteen-year-old kid who had fiddled with the controls on the car. The kid's screams of protest at the unjust actions of father were quite loud and contrasted rather sharply with the moans and groans from the bedroom. Bluntly stated this was an accident scene where it was really hard to keep a straight face as you did your duty.

I believe I failed miserably.

And then thrill of thrills, since it was an accident with injuries, I was required to give Troop I radio an accident report by radio for the news media. Try explaining the circumstances of this accident over the radio and, never mind, you don't want to try that. Eventually, I succeeded and I could hear laughter in the background in the Troop I radio room. With my duties for this accident completed I drove out of the trailer court just as fast as I could.

When people say the earth moved, this is not what they're talking about

10 PHOTOGRAPHY SCHOOL

During the early years of my career in Pulaski County, all of the troopers stationed here were constantly working criminal cases right and left. And if you worked a case and made an arrest, it was expected that you would be able to prove your case in court.

Here's where we had a little problem, rarely would we be able to get a photographer to document some of the details of the crime that would help you win the court case. I decided that I was going to take the extra step on my cases. I went to a pawn shop on the spur and bought a used 35mm reflex camera and ordered a book on how to take pictures.

I then entered into a period of time, a year or two, where I would constantly take photographs at crime scenes, have the photos developed, and try to figure out what I did wrong in order to improve for the next round. This trial and error process went on for two or maybe three years. Many times I found myself off duty at somebody else's crime scene taking photographs.

My photography obsession sort of resolved itself one fine day when I learned of a double homicide, in a trailer, less than a mile from my own residence. I was quickly on the scene taking photographs.

And then disaster! While concentrating on taking a photograph, I backed up a couple of steps, without looking behind me. I crashed into the official I&I photographer who was there to record the scene. Back in the old days, I&I stood for the Intelligence and Investigation unit. Basically the forerunners of the current Division of Drug and Crime Control usually referred to as DDCC.

In plain words, the I&I were the detectives of the Highway Patrol. The grizzled old sergeant from I&I turned around and gave me a dirty look. Since I was there off duty, and had not been officially called to the scene, and being a very low ranking patrol member, I quickly remembered that I had to go see a guy about a dog on the other side of town. I disappeared from the scene.

The next day, however, I got a call from the grizzled old sergeant, a very friendly tone of voice call. After a moment or so of chitchat, he asked me how my pictures turned out. I swear the devil made me say it because my words were, "Better than yours." And it turned out that I was correct.

Grizzled old Sarge had taken the establishing shot of the outside of the trailer and then had failed to throw some kind of a switch on his camera to a different position. As a result, he went to a double homicide and came back without a single picture of the inside of the trailer or of the victims of the crime. Massive failure.

In a rare display of tact for me, and trying to recover from my earlier devil statement, I quickly apologized for having only taken eighteen photographs before leaving the scene. I offered him my eighteen color photographs in size 8 x 10 to be delivered within the hour if he would like them.

Grizzled old Sarge thought that was a pretty good idea. If you are ever in a position to review the case file on this particular homicide investigation, you will note that the photographs were taken by grizzled old Sarge and little old me.

But this also had an upside for me. As the word of this little fiasco got around through the grapevine, I suddenly found that I was now welcome at just about any scene I walked into with my camera. In addition, several Troopers and some local officers started calling me out for photographic assistance. As a result, my photographs began showing up in more and more court cases and I realized I had another problem.

If I were called to the witness stand to testify as to the taking of the photographs at the crime scene and the defense attorney was to inquire as to my professional credentials I had the feeling that saying, "Well, I went to a pawn shop and bought a camera, then I bought a book to learn how to use the camera," was probably not going to be what the court would want to hear that day.

I began making application to attend the patrol's two-week basic crime scene photography school. I kept getting turned down.

And then, one day, a personnel situation arose where Sarge knew that my feelings would be hurt to a degree and he came to me asking me if there was anything he could do to make me feel better. I said, "Yes, I would like to go to photography school."

Sarge said, "You'll be in the next class." And so I was.

Opening day, hour number one of crime scene photography school, the old-timers who were teaching the class came into the room. They gave us students a speech telling us that, as a crime scene photographers, there was no telling what we would be called out to record and you better be prepared for these tests of your ability.

The lead instructor told us that, in order to give us a better idea of what we could be facing in the future, they were going to show us a montage of photographs that had been taken around the state. They hoped that these actual crime scene photographs would give us a better idea of what we could face in the future and would aid in our training.

They began flashing photographs on the screen. When photograph number eight popped up on the screen, I thought it looked familiar. Real familiar, in fact I raised my hand and kind of pointed toward the screen.

The instructor immediately said, "Yes JB that is your photograph and there are several more of your photographs in this presentation so sit back and shut up."

So in order to get my photography credentials for the witness stand, I went to basic photography school were they used some of my past photographs from actual crime scenes to help train me how to take pictures of actual crime scenes for the future. Which came first, the chicken or the egg?

However, I should make it plain that it was an excellent school and I learned tons of tricks about taking photographs at crime scenes. I now had some credentials for court. Three guesses who never ever had to testify as to his credentials for taking crime scene photographs in court?

Postscript: How do you explain the requirements of crime scene photographs to the person who is not a police officer? In my view the simple way is to say that you are using photographs to tell a story. You as a parent do much the same thing with your child's first birthday party. You don't want to miss a detail so you take pictures of him blowing out candles on the cake. Or reaching into the cake and grabbing a handful of cake to throw about. And so you document the whole party for later viewing. Every detail.

This is the same thing with a crime scene, you are documenting the story for much later viewing preferably in court. But instead of a cute pictures of a child blowing out candles, your crime scene shot might be the massive entry wound from a 12Ga. shotgun blast into a victim's chest. You document every detail you can see that would help in understanding the crime at a much later date. There are also some legal requirements you need to document, but that explanation would require another book. So just tell the story of the crime with pictures.

11 BACK UP TRUCKERS

Once upon a time, in days of old, there existed a magic period of time on the good old I-44 racetrack when truckers and Smokies exchanged many comments on the Citizens Band Radio. And that brought back a little memory of an incident where............

It was a nice and quiet overnight shift. I was the only Trooper on duty for probably fifty miles or more and I was chatting away on CB channel 19 with a couple of drivers who were following me west on I-44, being careful not to pass me, and thoughtfully warning all eastbound truckers of my location when.................

One of the drivers behind me said, "Well, Smoky, it's been fun talking to you, but you are about to get real busy when that car that just blew me off the road catches up to you."

And shortly thereafter, a big old station wagon car went zooming by me, with the driver half asleep and well over the posted sign suggestion about vehicle speeds........and just before stopping the car I ran the plate and...........Hit! Stolen vehicle! Taken in a burglary!.........So I told the driver that he was right, stolen car, be busy guys.

When the car did finally stop, we were alongside of one of those real deep ravines on I-44 just west of the Berean Church. Two guys bailed out of the car and jumped over the guardrail, on the run, down the hill, with me in foot pursuit. It was 2:00 a.m. or so and it was dark down there at the bottom of the ravine and somebody I know got real nervous in the dark.

Within just a minute or so, I was aware of a great commotion above me on I-44. Rather quickly, a small herd of truck drivers, on foot, came over the embankment headed down my way. And many of them were carrying metal objects that made the pew, pew, pew, type sounds that were not used as tire thumpers.

We soon found one bad guy laying on the ground with a fallen Cedar tree pulled over on top of him. When I got my prisoner to the top of the hill, I found, no exaggeration, at least 25 tractor trailer units stopped on both sides of I-44 with no drivers. I put my prisoner in the back seat of my patrol car and two drivers, who only had real tire thumpers, volunteered to see to it that he did not leave my car when I went back over the hill.

Flash forward a few more hours; our mini-manhunt has failed, I have directed traffic and cleared the I-44 roadblock. I have deposited my prisoner in the Pulaski County Crossbar Hotel, otherwise known as the county jail. I am back on the hunt for #2 runner once again. About 6:00 a.m., another driver going east called me on the CB and told me about a westbound hitchhiker who was almost to the truck stop at the 145mm exit. I had no problem taking a very tired, dehydrated, tick infested runner into custody.

And later that morning, my zone Sergeant chewed me out for not calling for backup during this incident. I tried very hard to explain to him that I had more backup then I could handle and our success rate had been 100%. He was not impressed..

12 RUBY'S TAVERN

Pulaski County, and police work in general, has a darker side and I'd be remiss if I didn't include some of those stories in this book as well. This story has a little of both, but the comic relief doesn't come until the end. Read on....

During the night of October 1, 1996, Thomas Stewart was shot to death by Alis Ben Johns on Missouri Rt. KK in Pulaski County Missouri. Local law enforcement officers were able to make a case on Johns and a warrant for his arrest was issued. As the winter months slowly passed by, Johns was able to evade capture.

On Feb. 7, 1997, as Ron Wilson returned home from work, he found Johns on his front porch with a shotgun he had just stolen from Wilson's house. John's fired one shotgun round into the ceiling of the home and one shot at Wilson which missed.

On Feb. 26, Johns forcibly entered the home of Bud and Melinda Veverka and held them at gunpoint, while he stole various items from their home. When Johns fled the scene of this burglary, he left the couple behind unharmed.

On Feb. 28, law enforcement officers, hunting for Johns in a rural section of Camden County, found the body of Leonard Voyles in his home, with a single fatal gunshot wound to the head. The officers were able to make a second murder case on Johns.

On March 9, law enforcement officers, who were still hunting Johns, in the heavily wooded rural area which formed a triangle with parts of Pulaski, Camden and Miller counties, found the body of Wilma Bragg in her home, with two gunshot wounds to the head. Once again, Johns was implicated in the crime.

At this stage of the manhunt, there were several hundred officers per day from multiple jurisdictions who had converged on the area of the heavily wooded three county triangle looking for Johns. A law enforcement command post was set up at the now vacant home of Leonard Voyles. Along with the officers involved in the manhunt, a horde of news media personal also descended upon the command post for daily media briefs.

Just a few miles to the south of the command post, the city of Richland Missouri also occupied a tri-border area. While most of the city is located in Pulaski County, smaller sections of the city lie in Camden County and Laclede County. It would be fair to state, that due to the violence displayed by Johns and the hundreds of officers constantly in the immediate area, the city of Richland was on a high alert status around the clock, waiting for the next explosion of violence.

And then on March 17, 1997, a white male matching John's description burst into Ruby's Tavern at a location inside the Richland City limits, within Laclede County. The man began to wave a gun around and threatened violence and mayhem towards the patrons of the tavern. Several calls for help were received by the police and the command post dispatched manhunt officers to the scene to aid the local officers, who were handling the usual police related calls during the manhunt.

And now we will switch gears so to speak. At the time

of this incident I was a Corporal with the Missouri State Highway Patrol assigned to Zone 4, the Pulaski County Zone of Troop I, headquartered at Rolla, Missouri. On March 17th, I was the ranking supervisor on duty, in Pulaski County that day, with the responsibility for handling the "routine" calls that occur on a daily basis and to assist the Johns manhunt officers as needed. What you are about to read is my personal view of what happened that day, my own thoughts and fears as the situation unfolded in front of me.

Most of the city of Richland lies within Pulaski County, but as a State Trooper I had statewide jurisdiction, so it did not matter when the Troop I radio division sent myself and Trooper D. Mark Hedrick running code three to the scene of Ruby's Tavern for the "man with a gun" call. Upon arrival, I counted at least six other police vehicles on scene. Before we had time to blink or try to understand what had happened, I found myself and Tpr. Hedrick standing at the open rear door of the tavern confronting a man holding a gun in one hand and a telephone handset in the other hand. And thus began my nineteen minute nightmare.

The man was talking on the phone. It was a wall mounted rotary phone with a phone cord that seemed to be twenty-five feet long. He was standing behind the bar when we arrived. Standing at the open door, I had a Remington 870 pump shotgun pointed at him and Tpr. Hedrick had a Glock .40 caliber pistol aimed at him. At the open front door of the tavern, on a diagonal line from our position, stood at least three other officers looking in at the subject with aimed weapons.

I began to try and talk to the man to see if I could talk him into a peaceful surrender. My effort was frustrated by the overhead presence of a very noisy helicopter and the fact that he was talking to somebody on the phone. The man was annoyed by my talking attempts and he pointed his firearm directly at us. The first of many such direct threats he would make that day.

The next few minutes were a stalemate, but during that time, we were able to determine that he had not yet fired the gun and nobody had been hurt so far in the incident. All of the patrons of the tavern had escaped. The man was in there by himself. And even better during his last act of aiming the gun at us, he had turned and directly faced us for the first time. The man was not Alis Ben Johns. He also appeared to be highly intoxicated and was very belligerent.

During the stalemate period of time, additional events occurred as more and more officers arrived on the scene and the news media horde, that had been at the manhunt command post when the call came out, were now on scene with us. A crew from KY-3 TV news station in Springfield, Missouri, was filming into the tavern, through the open front door, over the shoulders of the officers crouching at the door, and they captured the silhouette of the gunman against the back wall of the tavern, with the gun plainly shown in his hand.

A second TV cameraman from KSPR-33 news, also based out of Springfield, Missouri, was laying on the ground about ninety feet behind us with his camera pointed at the back door. This man was behind a concrete wall and my first thought upon seeing him there was that he was the smartest S. O. B. on the scene, the concrete wall was thick.

After we requested the helicopter to depart the area, we could talk more efficiently with the suspect. But he was still talking on the phone with somebody and that was creating problems. I would not find out until the following day that he was talking to a dispatcher at the Laclede County Sheriff's Office who actually knew him and who was also trying to get him to surrender. We began to make progress and he finally, after many long minutes, started to walk toward us with that very long phone cord, still talking on the phone, and when he hit the end of the cord, he stopped dead in his tracks. We had also retreated as he advanced and were now about thirty feet or so away from the door.

Then fate intervened. The wind blew the back door shut and we lost sight of him. The officers at the front door later told us that, as he turned around to go back to the bar, it appeared that he saw the officers at the front door for the first time. He fired seven shots at those officers.

We immediately opened the back door and saw him keeling down and trying to put another magazine into his firearm. The next second, I found myself lying on top of him behind the bar, as we fought for control of his gun, which was now on the floor somewhere underneath us.

My first thought was, "how did I get here? What the hell did I do?" And then another officer reached in under us and took possession of the firearm. The suspect was handcuffed and removed from the scene. He went to the Laclede County Jail.

As the suspect was led away, another officer asked me why I had charged him. I had no answer. I did not remember charging him. I still do not remember charging him so many years later. No recall of any part of the event. Not then, not now, and I suspect not never ever.

As I stood there extremely confused and very upset, the news media swarmed me for live interviews. Not a good time or position for an interviewee who was pumped up and full of adrenaline, but I did my best public relations bit for two news crews and then I stumbled off looking for a place to hide. But that did not work either. Troop I radio found me and gave me a major injury accident on the Texas County-Pulaski County boundary line about 30 miles away from Ruby's Tavern and I had to go back to work.

The aftermath of this incident, the comic relief, started with a laugh, a very badly needed laugh. The major auto accident with several injuries caused me to work several hours of overtime and when I, at long last, made it home my five year old son, who had spent the day in kindergarten class met me at the front door.

His first words were, "Hi dad! I hear you kicked ass today!"

That one floored me, so I asked him why he said that and he told me he had overheard a couple of the teachers at school talking about me and something I had done and that was what he remembered. Be careful out there people, little ears are listening.

After the laugh, the rest of the evening did not go very well. The suspect had pointed a firearm at me some dozen or more times while stating he was going to kill me. Why had I not fired? I had gambled my life and considering the seven shots fired at the officers at the front door, I had also gambled their lives by my lack of action, when directly confronted with the threat. Why? I found no answer that night nor have I found one since.

Our scenario was on par with many other incidents that officers have faced over the years and in today's world they often get criticized for not using a Taser, or shooting the gun out of his hand or some other equally dumbass idea usually presented by some person who would never place themselves into such a situation of their own free will. But the bottom line is that, while I was quite happy I did not have to explain to my five year old son I had killed a gunman with my shotgun, I was still left with doubts about my performance under pressure and those seven fateful shots that missed.

My second problem was worse. For years I had prided myself on my officer safety procedures and here I suddenly had a dozen officers asking me WHY? Or telling me HOW!!!.......... I had charged down the barrel of a loaded gun held by a man who had just shot at other officers. Why? I could not answer because I could not remember. The mental strain was immense.

Roughly three weeks of no sleep just about ruined me,

and then in response to my inquiry, the beautiful people at the KSPR-33 newsroom sent me a copy of their complete video coverage of the back door at Ruby's Tavern. And there on the video I saw myself clearly size up the situation when the door opened. I saw myself take a half step forward, pause, size up the situation again, another half step, pause, size up and then CHARGE!

Relief, the only word to describe the video. I could sleep again. As I write these words now, I still do not remember charging the suspect, butt stroking the gun out of his hand with my shotgun, and then doing my best imitation of an NFL tackle, but the proof is on the video. I can live with that proof, even though I do not remember the charge.

My first problem, however, is still with me. He pointed the gun directly at me at least a dozen times. I had the legal justification to fire in self-defense and end the situation. I did not do that and three officers at the front door had seven live rounds sent their way. Had one of them been hit by a bullet............well, I do not know what my actual feelings would have been that day since they were not harmed, but just thinking about it stirs up enough emotion to scare me. I hope I am never in such a situation again.

Not quite one month after the incident at Ruby's Tavern occurred, officers flushed Alis Ben Johns from a home he was burglarizing. Johns came out with his arm wrapped around a supposed hostage's head and with a gun to her head. The officers took immediate action to stop the crime and Johns was dropped to the ground via gunfire. The "hostage" who turned out to be his girlfriend was not harmed.

Johns has since been convicted in multiple Missouri counties on multiple heavy felonies and was spared the death penalty because he was "mentally retarded." He should never get out of the Missouri Department of Corrections.

Pictured from left to right are Colonel Weldon L. Wilhoit, J.B. King and his wife, Cheryl, when J.B. was presented his Medal of Valor.

What happened to the suspect from Ruby's Tavern? I do not know. I was never called to testify in his case and I never had the urge to check and find out. I am not sure why I felt that way, but I did and I have no regrets for not asking about his fate.

A little over one year after the incident at Ruby's Tavern occurred, the Missouri State Highway Patrol awarded me the Medal of Valor at the Patrol's annual awards ceremony banquet. It was the only Valor Medal awarded by the Patrol for the year 1997. Yes, I am quite proud of that achievement. There have only been a handful of valor medals awarded by the Patrol over the years and my name has been added to a very special group of Troopers.

After I retired from the Patrol in 2001, I found myself running for an elected position as the sheriff of Pulaski County Missouri. Be careful what you file for you may win the election. I served two four year terms as Sheriff. If you look at the photograph with this story, you will be able to see a bright blue bar with a gold "V" above my shirt pocket. That is the Valor Bar and is worn to signify the wearer has been awarded the Medal of Valor. The actual Valor Medal is never worn on the uniform. Maybe I should not have worn a valor bar issued by the Highway Patrol on a Sheriff's uniform shirt, but I did when I was Sheriff and my current Sheriff has given me permission to continue to wear the bar.

I have since retired as the elected Sheriff. I still have a commission as a deputy sheriff and I still assist the detective division of the Pulaski County Sheriff's office as an unpaid reserve officer.

In retirement, I have returned to my hobby of history and journalism. My first book, "The Tilley Treasure", published in 1984, tells the story of an actual civil war buried treasure that was found in Pulaski County in 1962.

J.B. King, in uniform, with his Valor bar above his name.

The book traces the money and the history of the family that buried the money. The book also recounts quite a lot of Missouri civil war history for a view of the civil war that is very different from the civil war most people visualize. "Tilley" has it all, buried treasure, a prisoner massacre, a spy story, guerrilla marauders running all over the hills and many other civil war items of interest.

My second book "Justice", first published in 2004, combines my interest in civil war history with my law enforcement background. Justice explores the history of Union Army military tribunals and court-martials. Besides explaining the concept and procedure for these trials Justice gives you many pages of actual testimony from the trial transcripts of seven selected case. These cases range from a violation of an oath of allegiance to the theft of a cavalry mount to murder. During the civil war, the Union Army executed 267 of their own men. Two of those cases are covered in Justice. In six of the cases documented in Justice that ended with a guilty verdict, the verdict was appealed up the military chain of command and finally stopped at the desk of the Commander in Chief, President Abraham Lincoln. The decision by President Lincoln proved to be the final answer for each defendant. The documents Lincoln signed are shown in the book.

Those books are a different tone than this one, as this one is about my personal experiences. There are more books to come that are from my own experience, stay tuned.

13 SHOOTING AT THE SHERIFF'S OFFICE

Throughout this book, I have tried to present stories with a little humor in them. This will not be one of those stories. Rather it will be a brief story of a three day manhunt event that has mostly been forgotten here in Pulaski County due to the passage of time.

This event was about as serious as you can get in police work. In this particular case I was but one of many Troopers and police officers who were involved with this case. For this case, I had to go to the newspaper morgue files and consult front-page news articles to refresh my memory of the case. The details in this case are from the front page newspaper stories.

This particular case began on October 22, 1977, with a call from the Federal Bureau of Investigation to the Pulaski County Sheriff's Department giving them the location of a suspect generally known as Willie Taylor, age 24, from the state of Oklahoma. Taylor was wanted by the FBI and Oklahoma authorities as a suspect in the February 18, 1976, stabbing death of a Muskogee, Oklahoma, policeman. The Muskogee officer just happened to have been Taylor's brother-in-law.

Taylor was apprehended, without incident, and taken to the Pulaski County jail where he was placed in an interview room. FBI Agent Jim Holmes, who was one of three FBI agents stationed at the Fort Leonard Wood office of the FBI, was interviewing Taylor, when Pulaski County Deputy Sheriff Wayne Fritts entered the interview room.

Taylor lunged at Fritts and was able to jerk the deputy's revolver from his holster. Taylor then fired several shots, one of which struck Deputy Fritts in the back of the head. Agent Holmes briefly scuffled with Taylor before Taylor was able to shove him aside and run for the front door of the Sheriff's office. Agent Holmes fired one shot at Taylor as he went out the door.

According to the newspaper accounts, as Taylor went out the door, he pointed the revolver at Waynesville City Police Chief Fermin "Pappy" Raines and tried to fire a shot at him. The revolver did not fire. Taylor, who was barefoot, ran across the parking lot and disappeared behind some buildings. The manhunt was on.

Taylor successfully eluded local officers, until the following day, when he stole a pickup truck from a barn on the south side of I-44. While stealing this vehicle, Taylor pointed his weapon at three local men and was reported to have "growled" at one of the men. Taylor fled north on Highway 7 into Camden County. Following a brief vehicle pursuit in Camden County, Taylor ran into the woods and a manhunt began.

The following day, Taylor was flushed from some woods by police dogs and attempted to run from officers. As Taylor ran across an open field, a Missouri State Water Patrol Officer fired a single rifle shot at him which struck Taylor in the upper thigh. Taylor fell to the ground unconscious and the manhunt was over.

A federal grand jury sitting in Kansas City Missouri later returned an indictment against Taylor for two criminal counts relating to assaulting an FBI agent with a firearm.

As for Pulaski County Deputy Sheriff Wayne Fritts, he was treated and released from the Fort Leonard Wood Hospital for what a Sheriff's Department spokesman described as, "A deep graze", on the back of his head. A very lucky man.

Postscript: At the time of this incident I had known Wayne for many years. Even before he became a deputy. Hunting for somebody who has already killed one officer and then wounded your friend takes a lot out of you. It is a very emotional situation. You also know if you are the next officer to find this guy, you could get hurt bad. Somehow, in this manhunt, they kept sending me to the wrong patch of woods or the wrong barn to search for Taylor. But you don't know that the location is wrong until you complete your amped up search. I was quite happy to hear that the Water Patrol officer had dropped him.

In the aftermath of this case, in the years that followed, I must also confess that there is a slight possibility that I may have referred to Wayne as "Hardhead" once or twice or three times or.........

14 ABSENT WITHOUT LEAVE

The Missouri State Highway Patrol Training Academy had not prepared me for the Troop I, Zone 4, Pulaski County AWOL pursuit game. I barely remember them mentioning the fact that we could arrest AWOL's in the Academy. So when I got to Pulaski County during the first couple working days the senior Trooper's made sure to give me a little lecture on how to apprehend AWOL's. And then one night in that first week or so one of the senior Trooper's told us he had received information about the location of an AWOL soldier and we were going AWOL hunting.

Three of us drove to a nearby town, located the house in question, and I was sent to the back door of the house to make sure nobody left unexpectedly when the senior Troopers knocked on the front door. Nothing happened at the back door but I could hear little commotion inside and pretty soon the senior Trooper's yelled for me to come around front because they were ready to leave.

And standing there with the senior Trooper's was the AWOL soldier, the six-month pregnant AWOL soldier. The senior Trooper's loaded her into their vehicle and drove her to the Fort Leonard Wood MP desk and released her to the tender care and mercy of the United States Army. Case closed.

This chapter is a collection of AWOL stories, as I had occasion to be involved in many, especially in the early days.

As previously recounted, chasing AWOL military soldiers was practically a way of life for those of us working the Pulaski County zone. And this is another story of AWOL pursuit. This particular story started out with a telephone call to Troop I advising us that three AWOL's were walking east on the railroad track approaching Devil's Elbow.

We moved into position and caught the three men by surprise. We quickly had two of them in custody but AWOL number three had different plans for the day.

We spent the next hour chasing this guy round and round, over Hill, over Dale, through the valleys, and finally we had him cornered near the bank of the Big Piney River. At that point, with us closing in, he jumped in the river and swam across to the other side. This move on his part was totally unexpected.

This was January, the water was freezing, and we had snow on the ground. And now the soaking wet AWOL was charging up over the hill disappearing into the vast track of unoccupied land that was on the other side of the Big Piney River from where we stood. We never saw the guy again.

And to this day I have often wondered if he was able to survive the coming darkness, under the severe weather conditions that we had, and make it home safe and sound. Or did he die of exposure on some unknown ridge top in the forest and his skeleton is still waiting to be discovered? I suspect we will never know the answer to this particular puzzle, but as far as determination to avoid apprehension and a return to the military environment, this guy took first place in the contest. I just hope he did not have to pay a severe price for winning.

Soldiers going AWOL from Fort Leonard Wood created many problems for the local residents. And as a result many residents did not hesitate to call Troop I whenever they spotted a possible AWOL soldier walking along. One of the major traffic arteries for AWOL soldiers was the railroad spur that ran from Fort Leonard Wood back toward Rolla, Missouri. The local rumor mill on Fort Leonard Wood let all of the soldiers know that the railroad right-of-way was a straight arrow pointed east toward the civilization of the bigger cities in the state of Missouri. And as such reports of AWOL soldiers walking east on the railroad tracks were extremely common.

On this particular day shift, Troop I was notified that there was an AWOL on the tracks headed east. I moved into position near our favorite ambush spot for surprising the AWOL's. This was a railroad trestle over a county road. If you played your cards right, and officers cut off both ends of the bridge simultaneously, while the AWOL soldiers were on the bridge, they had a choice of walking up to you or jumping over the trestle and falling about 100 feet straight down. They usually walked up to you and surrendered. However, after I waited a while at this ambush spot nothing happened.

I decided that the time element was wrong on this sighting report and I went to ambush spot number two, which was a railroad crossing just inside Phelps County. Leading up to the railroad crossing, the AWOL soldiers would be a caught in the railroad crossing, surrounded by high embankments on both sides. If the officer came over the embankment, just before they got to the railroad crossing, on Route P, then he could surprise the soldiers and usually was able to take them into custody.

So I parked my patrol car behind the embankment and

waited. Soon, I could hear voices on the railroad tracks and I charged up and over the hill all by myself. I found myself looking at nine AWOL soldiers. I only had six rounds in my revolver and when the soldier's saw me they charged at me en mass.

I was in trouble, but when the soldiers got close enough to talk to me their first words were questions such as, do you have a car? Where is the car? Is the car warm?

I quickly realized that these nine soldiers going AWOL had clearly been out at least one night in the January temperatures, that were quite low, and it was also fairly obvious that they were not adequately dressed to handle such low temperatures. Or to put it more bluntly they were freezing to death and they saw me as their Savior.

I ended up putting nine AWOL soldiers in my Ford Crown Vic patrol car and driving back to Fort Leonard Wood to surrender them back to the MPs. During the ride, I kept my handgun underneath my left leg where they could not reach it, I made sure they all understood that it was there, and, at this range, I could not miss. But that was a statement that was not needed because it became quite clear that the only thing on their mind was food and a warm place to land.

The soldiers uniforms were saturated with the smell of wood smoke from the fires they had built overnight to try and stay warm and in the confined quarters of my patrol car the smoke smell positively caused my eyes to water. I was quite happy when we finally arrived at the MP headquarters on Fort Leonard Wood and I was able to turn the nine soldiers over to the AWOL apprehension team. Case closed.

Here we have the story of the AWOL Houdini. This story is the story of another great AWOL chase. It happened a long time ago in the early 1970's and for some reason I cannot remember how we came into contact with this particular AWOL the first time. I know that I and another Trooper had picked him up and we took him to the Fort Wood MP desk. During the trip to the MP desk, the AWOL told us he hated the damn Army and he would go AWOL again.

So when we got to the MP desk, we told the desk Sergeant about his lousy attitude toward the military. The good desk Sergeant assured us they would take care of that issue. Before we could clear the main gate leaving post, we were notified that the AWOL had escaped from the MP building by using a broom.

My partner immediately asked, "Did he use it to fly?"

And so the morning after we were notified that he had escaped, it was a rainy cloudy day in Waynesville, Missouri. As I drove past a business on Highway 17, in the middle of the main drag in Waynesville, I became aware that the thoroughly soaked fella standing on the sidewalk to my right was our missing AWOL and he was staring right at me.

The same Trooper from the day before was right behind me and, as the two of us got out of our cars to make the arrest, the AWOL began running. We chased the AWOL for several city blocks. The suspect was heading across the square in Waynesville more or less in the direction of the Waynesville post office. At the last second, he veered to his left and tried to run across the street to the medical complex. At that time a passing motorist who saw the AWOL running with two troopers in hot foot pursuit took matters into his own hands and tried to run over the AWOL with his car.

The AWOL soldier was able to dodge the car, but in doing so, he lost his balance and tripped over onto the sidewalk. I landed on top of him and a second or so later the second Trooper landed on top of us. We handcuffed the AWOL subject and we started back to Fort Wood with him. While we were in route to Fort Leonard Wood, the AWOL kept telling us that as soon as he got on post he was going to desert again. He was not staying in the Army under any circumstance.

I asked him how many times he had gone AWOL and been caught. His answer was five times now. Shame on me, but I told the AWOL that he was an idiot. That all he was going to have to do was stay put for two to three weeks and give the Army time to process his paperwork and that they would kick him out of the Army with a bad conduct discharge.

He asked me if I was kidding and I said no. I repeated my detailed instructions on how to get his bad conduct discharge and he said thank you. We delivered him to the MP desk and we never heard of him again. I assume he got his bad conduct discharge and was kicked out of the Army. Case closed.

Another interesting AWOL case involved a case of alleged mistaken identity. For this call I found myself responding to the mom-and-pop convenience store located on I-44 at Route Z in Devil's Elbow, better known as the Piney Runts place. Inside the store was an AWOL soldier dressed in military clothing with a head shaved down to fuzz and a sour look on his face. I proceeded to tell him that you're going home, back to Fort Wood sonny.

And then he told me a wild tale. He said he was from Indiana and he had been picked up by mistake by the local law enforcement agency, who mistook him for his nearly identical cousin, who was AWOL from the Army and the local law enforcement had turned him over to an MP detail in Indiana which had sent him to Fort Leonard Wood. He said it'd taken a couple weeks before he finally got the attention of the Colonel in his particular military unit and told him the story. He said that the good Colonel had investigated the story and found out it was true. So this morning they had released him from the military base and he was trying to hitchhike back to Indiana.

I congratulated him on the best AWOL avoidance's story I had ever heard. Especially the part were a full bird Colonel had investigated his claim. I then took him back to the Fort Wood MP desk. However, before I could leave, the desk sergeant said, "Hold on a second the duty officer wants to talk to you."

When the duty officer for the day shift showed up, we chatted and the upshot of the chatter was that, every word the kid had told me was true. There had been a horrible screw-up by the authorities in Indiana followed by a further screw-up by the military authorities and they had held him captive at Fort Wood for a couple weeks before they got it straightened out. He had been released from the base this morning with their best wishes.

I picked up my new friend from the MP desk and we headed east on the interstate, considerably further east than he had gotten on his first try. I then handed him over to another Trooper, with a quick explanation of the circumstances and a request that the next Trooper unofficially relay him east as far as he could. I don't know if that Trooper was able to hand him off to another Trooper and really cut down the distance that he had to go to Indiana but I sure hope that happened.

My last AWOL story had an odd turn that happened 48 years later. Although I am now retired from the Missouri State Highway Patrol, I am still reserve deputy sheriff with the Pulaski County Sheriff's Department and the radio operators at Troop I are well aware of that fact. As a consequence, whenever they receive a call from somebody requesting historical information about Pulaski County or an inquiry of a criminal nature back in the early 1970's or 1980's, when an answer is not immediately forthcoming from the patrol's computer system, the person calling is frequently referred to me for possible answers.

And so on May 15, 2018, I received a message from

Troop I dispatch asking me to call a man in Wisconsin. He was looking for information on the death of his AWOL brother in Pulaski County, Missouri. I called the man as soon as I got the message and I asked him what information he could give me about his brother's death.

The man told me that the Army told him his brother had gone AWOL and that evidently he had been hit by a car on the outer road near the trailer court where his wife was staying. The man told me that this had occurred on May 15, 1970. I asked him for the name of the trailer court and he told me it was the Pulaski Estates Trailer Court. He told me the Army said his brother was seen in the ditch by a passing truck driver.

OMG! On this date, 48 years, ago I had been standing in the road ditch between the westbound lane of I-44 and the North Outer Road just a few yards short of the Pulaski Estates Trailer Court looking at a body in the median that was hidden by tall weeds. The body had been spotted by a passing truck driver on I-44. The victim was a GI who was listed as AWOL. He had been hit by an unknown car several days before. The May heat had not been gentle to his body.

And so I was able to give the man some details of the case and more importantly, I told him where to call to find the rest of the details. I had not played a really active part in this investigation because, at the time it occurred, I had only been working in Pulaski County for four months and fifteen days. But I was able to give the man some closure and I believe I did help him..

15 THE BROKEN BONE BANK ROBBERY

There are no secrets in Pulaski County. Rumor control may get the facts a little garbled, but it will not be a secret. Therefore as many of you already know since retiring from office as your Sheriff I have managed to trip over my clumsy feet a couple of times and have broken a number of bones. As a result of these frequent smashing falls, one of my friends recently asked me in a very sarcastic tone of voice, "Did you ever break a bone while working for the Highway Patrol?".

And the answer to that question is yes, as a matter of fact I did, and so today we will tell the story of JB's broken bone. But it's a story that covers a little more territory than just a broken bone. And unlike previous stories of this nature, today I will name names and if you see a name it's correct. I will also leave out a number of colorful four letter words that were used on this occasion. And so our story begins…………..

Once upon a time in Pulaski County Missouri, January 29, 1980, to be precise, I was working a day shift on a nice clear January day. I was also about three weeks into my first ever assignment as a Field Training Officer (FTO) and with me on this date was the new nugget rookie, straight from the Missouri State Highway Patrol Academy, a man many locals will know, Trooper Kirby Johnson.

Kirby and I had just walked out of the Deville Texaco Service Station in St. Robert when we saw the other day car heading westbound on the city route with his light bar turning and burning. No siren sounds, just the light bar activated, so we called him on the radio and asked what was up. And his answer was alarm sounding at the First State Bank of St. Robert. The time was just a minute or two before 8 AM.

At this point, I should probably mention that fate had dealt Kirby and I a rather unkind hand the day before. While going through the car wash, the machinery had broken the scanner antenna off of my vehicle, and as a result we could not hear the radio traffic from the St. Robert Police, Waynesville City Police, and the Pulaski County Sheriff's Department. On this date, that was a rather critical equipment failure.

Now back to the story. As part of the FTO training, you are given a large notebook full of tasks and jobs and assignments for which it is your responsibility to make sure that the new rookie trooper performs every one of these tasks in a satisfactory fashion. One such scenario was a hold up alarm in progress call. On this date in history, I made one of the best command decisions that I ever made, because while in route to the bank, I assured Trooper Johnson that although this would be a false alarm at 8 AM in the morning caused by an employee who fumbled with their entry code, we were going to treat it like it was real and we were going to act like it was real.

Just a minute or so later, we found ourselves at the back door of the bank, both of us were down behind a concrete wall covering the back door, and we were the only two officers at the rear of the bank. At this point, I should mention that the statute of limitations has expired on certain old offenses and I will confess, that when given the FTO assignment, I realized that we were only going to have one shotgun for two officers. So that raised the question of, when the brown stuff was flying through the air toward the whirling fan blades, should the veteran officer get the .12gauge or should the rookie officer get the .12gauge? And I will confess that I did not like either answer and so somehow a non-issue, unauthorized, chunk of wood and metal, with a thirty round magazine attached, that gave a great deal of comfort to the holder during risky situations , had somehow found its way into my patrol car.

Thus we are at the back door; Trooper Johnson was pointing a shotgun at the back door looking straight in the door and I am off to the right with my unauthorized chunk of metal looking at the side of the back door. Nothing much was happening, other than a parking problem was starting to develop in the front part of the bank parking lot. It appeared that every on-duty Waynesville City Police Officer, St. Robert City Police Officer, and all of the on-duty deputies, were all in the front parking lot and we were starting to get off- duty guys driving into the parking lot and jumping out of their cars. It began to look like somebody was going to have to direct traffic at the front of the bank, but Kirby and I were still by ourselves at the back of the bank.

And then in a blink of an eye, things changed. I looked toward the front parking lot and saw the other Trooper running away from the bank clutching a shotgun, bent over at the waist, and as he got to his patrol car he sort of swan dived over the car into a hiding position behind said patrol car. The cold voice in the back of my mind immediately said, "Missouri troopers don't run like that unless........." And my conscious being said, "No, no, no, that can't be this is a false alarm." And the cold voice in the back of my head said, "Hey stupid Missouri troopers don't run like that unless..........."

So I used my portable extender radio to call Troop I

and I told them that something was wrong here, start the backup. For the next several minutes, nothing happened. I was standing there mortified by the fact that in my first FTO assignment, with my brand-new rookie by my side at a false alarm, I had just called for backup. I was never going to live this one down. And then the back door opened and Trooper Johnson immediately pointed his shotgun at the door and yelled, "Y'all freeze!"

At that point, my attention was drawn to the two ladies walking out of the back door of the bank. Now I should also confess that this was my bank and I knew both of the ladies on a first name basis as tellers who worked at my bank. So I immediately looked toward Trooper Johnson and yelled, "Kirby they work here!"

As my attention returned to the back door of the bank, my first question was, "Hey wait a second who are these two black guys wearing the coveralls walking out behind the tellers?........"

"Oh FUDGE! This is for real, this is a bank robbery!!!!!"

Trooper Johnson, meanwhile, told the men to get down on their faces on the parking lot and they complied. As they laid down, the two ladies stepped to one side and I could then see that they were both holding firearms in their left hands, the side of their body that had been away from me, but in a direct line with Trooper Johnson's vision.

With the two gentlemen in the jumpsuits lying on the ground in the concrete parking lot, Trooper Johnson immediately jumped his concrete wall and approached them. My first thought was that I have to protect my rookie..........so I jumped my concrete wall......... well, not exactly, my foot caught near the top of the wall and I came down face first on the concrete parking lot, with my right hand extended way out in front of me, with a certain rather heavy unauthorized hunk of wood and metal in my hand, which immediately karate chopped my right thumb between said unauthorized object and the concrete parking lot. Or in simpler terms JB just broke his right thumb.

Within a matter of seconds, Kirby and I had the bad guys handcuffed and the situation was under control. Then we were nearly trampled by a herd of officers that had been at the front of the bank who were now running to the rear of the bank. I used my radio to tell Troop I that we had two in custody, that we did not know where the getaway vehicle was, and to halt the backup on I-44 in place. Upon hearing me say that, a municipal officer who will not be named went over to the bad guys and said, "Boy, where's the getaway car?"

Even more surprising, the bad guy rolled over and said, "White Ford van with the engine running it's on the I-44 ramp right over there." And so we left the bank and swarmed the ramp, and sure enough there was a white Ford van with Texas plates, with the engine running and nobody in the vehicle. We now had total victory in our grasp.

And much as I hate to embarrass my good friend, the other Trooper, whose name I seem to have left out of the story somehow, yes he did. He walked up to the front of the bank and looked in the window to see what was going on inside and there about ten inches away from him was a bank robber looking out the same window to see what was going on outside. Both men immediately ran for cover. Not sure which one was the most frightened.

So, on a day when we could not hear the municipal radio traffic, that we so desperately needed to hear, because they had broadcast this call as an actual armed robbery in progress, witnessed by people on the second floor of the bank and called in by those same people. Every other officer on the scene knew that this was a real bank robbery. Kirby and I, however, due to the broken scanner antenna, were off in La-La land. And thus my decision to treat it as real that day was a really smart decision. Moral of the story, somebody always fails to get the word.

And yes, about a half an hour after everything was secure at the bank, the pain in my right thumb was such that we drove to the old Pulaski County Hospital and the folks in the ER got to laugh at me while they x-rayed the thumb and applied the protective splints. Then it was back to St. Robert PD, where everybody was meeting to get this mess all squared away. And all the officers there got to laugh at me also. And now that I have written this story, which first appeared as a column in the local newspaper, the number of people who can laugh at me over this story just grew by quite a few numbers.

In the days, weeks and even years after bank robbery day, I found out a few more bits to the overall story I did not know. When I called in for backup, one of the Rolla Zone Troopers was in the radio room and heard the traffic. He promptly ran to his patrol car and backed up quickly from his parking space.......but unfortunately backed up a shade too far and found one of the very large posts that ringed the parking lot at Troop I at that time....Boom! Body damage to P-car.

A pair of Patrol detectives jumped into one car and headed for St. Robert. Somewhere around the Jerome hill in Phelps County they blew an engine belt on their car. Suspect excessive speed may have been a factor here and when they arrived at St. Robert Police HQ their car was surrounded by a large mountain of smoke and steam. But we did not need the St. Robert Fire Department.

In Jefferson City, at the Patrols Aircraft Division office located at the Jeff City airport, the phone rang and the only pilot there was told to "scramble" a unit for air support in Troop I. He ran out to his chopper and started flipping switches and just as the big overhead fan blades began the make those neat loud whoop, whoop, noises, he was advised to cancel. Situation under control.

Meanwhile, back at the bank, the bad guys had surveyed the bank parking lot while discussing the idea of shooting their way out of their jam and.............they decided there were too many of us around the bank. Next, they considered the hostage/negotiation route and they decided there were too many of us and we appeared somewhat disorganized..........so that plan went down the drain.

Realizing that the best course would be surrender, they went into the bank president's office and called their girlfriends in Texas and told them they would be out of circulation for a few days and would contact them again when their status had resolved. Then they took the two female tellers to the back door, forced their firearms, including a shotgun with most of the barrel cut off, into their hands and shoved them out the door first so the goofy cops could shoot them. But we did not play that game and concentrated on the bad guys.

And I should also confess that, once we had them in custody, Kirby and I entered the bank to sweep it clean of bad guys. I had only taken about five steps into the bank when I was tackled by a friend of mine who worked at the bank. Denise was scared and oh by the way she was about eight and a half months pregnant and she was HUGE! I do mean HUGE! She had me wrapped up in a bear hug and would not let go. As we waddled about looking for more bad guys, carrying my rifle became very awkward and I kept telling her to let go so I could look for more bad guys and she kept telling me, "No! There were only two of them." About twenty minutes later, Denise finally let go of me and sat down to rest. The good news here was we did not have to remember any of the fine points from the childbirth class.

If I remember correctly, after the FBI presented the case to the U. S. Attorney's office, both bad guys got a 15 year vacation at federal expense. That part of the story happened so fast, I think they were serving time before we finished typing our bank robbery reports. I am sure they enjoyed their stay as guests of the government.

16 DARK HUMOR

There is an old saying in the world that police officers have a black sense of humor. And there is some truth to that statement. When you deal with death, destruction, and misery on a daily basis you sometimes struggle to save your sanity. Then the black humor strikes. And the black humor can strike at really odd times, in really weird places, and under really weird circumstances. It can strike during times of high stress, while facing potential violence. For today's story we will deal with a black sense of humor that struck me in the middle of the John David Brown murder manhunt in Phelps County somewhere around April 4-5-6, 1987.

Brown was a prison escapee from the Fordland Correctional Center in Missouri, who was found by the Rolla City Police Department to be in possession of a stolen vehicle while staying at a Rolla motel. As they attempted to arrest Brown, he shot and wounded a Rolla City Police Officer, James "Jay" Horn the night of March 30, 1987. Brown escaped into the woods and the manhunt began. The manhunt would later be dubbed the largest and longest in Missouri history and it made national news.

And then April 1, 1987, Brown shot and killed church

caretaker, Claude Curtis Long, inside a church near Doolittle, Missouri, just outside of Rolla. This murder occurred right in the middle of the manhunt territory. The manhunt had been going for a very long week full of twelve hour shifts, and when you added the travel time and preparation time, the shifts were actually more like fifteen or sixteen hours per day. The officers assigned to the manhunt were getting very tired and we had a lot of ground to cover, measured in square miles, and we needed many more officers.

And so a solution was found, the Missouri governor called out the Missouri National Guard and we got a MP Company out of St. Clair, Missouri, to roll in like the Seventh Cavalry and save the day. On the first day of the MP deployment, we had what I will call the marriage ceremony. The Missouri State Highway Patrol Lieutenant and all the troopers, as well as other civilian police officers were in one big group, while across the room, the MP Lieutenant and all of the MP Officers were in another group. The patrol Lieutenant would call out a troopers name and he would step forth, the MP Lieutenant would call out a MP Officer's name and he would step forth, and the two officers were then united in a state of holy manhunt.

As I walked to my patrol car, accompanied by my new found battle buddy, a young fresh lean mean MP fighting machine, clutching his trusty .12gauge pump and with the classic model 1911 caliber .45 semiautomatic pistol on his hip, my thought was, "We are in great shape here to slay the dragon. Or arrest the Dragon; the decision to fight us or surrender to us was really up to John David Brown." We could accommodate him either way.

As we drove toward our assigned patrol grid, which was located deep in the heart of the area that John Brown was thought to be hiding in, I thought to myself that it was really good to have a partner for once and was extra good for us to be so fully loaded for bear. My thought was, "Just show your face John David Brown."

A few minutes later and a couple miles north of Troop I headquarters, my new friend, the lean mean MP fighting machine turned toward me and said, "Sir, oh Sir, do you know when they're going to issue us ammunition?"

"Wait, you don't have any ammunition?"

"No Sir, not a round."

Oh damn!

So a quick stop alongside the roadway, we step to the rear of my car and, from a small supply hidden in the trunk of my vehicle, I gave him a number of buckshot rounds for his .12gauge shotgun. I had to apologize for being fresh out of .45 ACP rounds on that date. Dealing with John David Brown was now a maybe proposition.

And then we were back on the road heading for the assigned patrol grid; me and my halfway armed lean semi-mean MP fighting machine. Another mile or so down the road and the young lad turns to me and said, "Sir, oh sir, I'm scared, I don't know what I'm doing, you see I'm a helicopter mechanic by MOS and I just transferred into this MP unit two weeks ago, I haven't had one minute worth of MP training."

My response was, "You're kidding right?"

No, he was not. So we pulled to the side of the road again for a quick conference on strategy and tactics. After several minutes of discussion, we arrived at a solution. The upshot of the solution was that he said he could follow orders and I assured him that if we went on a call he would hear orders. Then we sailed forth once again, but this time my thought was, "Please, dear Lord, do not let us find John David Brown."

We were once again headed toward our assigned patrol grid. When the lean, young, untrained, half way armed, MP fighting machine turned to me once again and said, "Sir, oh sir.......... (I was starting to hate that phrase)........ But this time he only needed a potty break and fortunately the big Cedar tree on the left side of the road was available.

And so with all business attended to, we finally arrived at our patrol area and spent the day looking for the elusive John David Brown. The truth be told, before the day was over, I recognized that my young lad was a valuable addition to have along, he listened carefully to orders and he carried them out exactly. We actually made a pretty good team that day.

The next morning, when the marriage ceremony took place again, the MP Lieutenant called out another man to accompany me that day and I told the MP Lieutenant I wanted my battle buddy from yesterday back because I knew what he would do in a pinch. The MP Lieutenant consented to my request and my helicopter mechanic and I went hunting for John David Brown one more uneventful day. This time he had ammo from the start. And we never saw John David Brown.

BUT, that would change for me in the summer of 2005 as I faced many challenges during my first year as the elected Sheriff of Pulaski County. John David Brown and I sat down at the same table and looked each other in the eye as we discussed an uncharged murder he committed here in Pulaski County in 1985.....................but that's a really long story for another day.

A really long story for another day, Yes! A book on the two John David Brown murder cases are in my plans for the future. I would have to research book one, the Rolla murder, but book two, the Pulaski County murder, was my own case. I have all the files and photos. And the inside track on how we got him to confess to the murder and plead guilty without a contested trial. Stay tuned for that one.

17 WHY YOU SHOULD ALWAYS HANDCUFF JESUS

I n this particular story, another Trooper is the main party involved. I had a minor secondary role in this particular case. My part of the story involved a visit to the Fort Leonard Wood Army Community Hospital Emergency Room that did not go well. Over the years with many, many, visits to the Fort Wood ER in the line of duty I will be the first to tell you that 99.5% of the time the doctors and nurses in the ER treated me like I owned the place. This story however is a story of the other .5% of the time.

The case started with Troop I radio dispatch reporting that a male subject was walking down the centerline of Highway 28 forcing cars off the road. One of the other Troopers was much closer than I was and he was on scene before I even got close. As soon as he got out of the car to confront the subject, the subject pulled out a large butcher knife and began slashing the knife at him as he advanced. Our Trooper retreated until he could retreat no more, the man refused to drop the knife and kept slashing it at the Trooper, and the Trooper shot him in the upper part of the leg.

When the bullet struck the subject, he stood for a second looking at the Trooper, and then he dropped the knife. The Trooper handcuffed him and called for assistance. When I arrived on the scene, I assumed the guard duty position over the suspect while the other Trooper obtained identification information from several people who had watched the subject chase the Trooper around his patrol car, waving the knife at him.

The Pulaski County Ambulance District sent a unit to the scene and they began treating the suspect. Since the suspect was a gunshot victim, and the Pulaski County Hospital was no longer operational, that meant he would be taken to the Fort Leonard Wood Hospital Emergency Room. By this time, the Troop I staff officer was on the scene and the Lieutenant ordered me to escort the suspect to the Fort Wood ER and maintain custody over him.

Upon our arrival at the Fort Wood Hospital, the suspect was wheeled into one of the treatment rooms of the ER. And then things started to go wrong. The military doctor on duty in the ER insisted that I take the handcuffs off the suspect so he could treat him. I refused. The Doctor being God in his ER and somewhat of a pompous ass made quite the scene. He seemed to completely fail to understand that the small peon that I was might actually know what I was doing and he failed to closely examine the idea of removing the cuffs. In any event, the doctor became quite vocal in his assertion that he could not treat the suspect until the handcuffs were off. So tempers flared a little bit. The doctor finally told me that this was a federal reservation and that I had no jurisdiction on it and he wanted the cuffs off of the suspect.

I told him that if you're going to put it that way, I will take the cuffs off the suspect.

My thinking at the time? "I hope you are the first guy he punches out!"

I made the suspect sit up on the ER table and I put

him in an arm bar hold, while I took the cuffs off. Once I had the cuffs in my hand, I released him from the arm bar hold and jumped backward several feet. The suspect then quietly laid back down on the table. The doctor and the nurses in the room gave me very dirty looks over my treatment of the poor injured suspect. They smiled as they stepped up to the table.

As they reached for the suspect to begin treatment, the suspect suddenly lunged forward on the ER table into a sitting position. He then held up his hand and surveyed the room with a really wild eyed look on his face.

He said, "I am Jesus Christ and I shall now perform one of my miracles."

The good doctor immediately looked at me and pointed to the handcuffs that I was still holding. He then pointed to the suspect. I told the good doctor, "I believe you mentioned that this is a federal reservation and I do not have the authority to handcuff him." I walked out of the room, but I stood guard near the door where I could see the suspect in case he tried to escape.

And he thought to himself, "Sorry, I don't get paid enough to restrain deities. Besides, it's going to take more than cuffs for this one. Looks, like you need a hammer and nails."

About three minutes later, a small herd of military police officers came running in the back door of the ER and went straight into the treatment room with the suspect. Later on, I got the chance and I explained the situation to the senior MP Officer who was there. He told me that they would take good care of the suspect until he was ready to be medically released. And, at that point he said, "Since he's a civilian, you can have him. And oh by the way he is bat shit crazy."

Postscript: For those readers who live and work in Pulaski County you should probably know that the good doctor was not exactly correct in his statement that I had no jurisdiction on post. If the crime is committed on post, he is correct, but if the crime is committed off post, he is wrong. The latest revision of the statutes that govern jurisdiction on Ft. Leonard Wood came about in 1978, when the state of Missouri and the Secretary of the Army cut a deal. And here is how it works.

The state of Missouri reserved the right to serve civil and criminal process on Ft. Wood. During the first month of each newly elected sheriff's term in office, he signs a memorandum of understanding between the sheriff, the Judge Advocate General's Office and the Office of the Provost Marshal as to how the process will be handled. The simple version of the process is as follows. Usually, on Monday, the sheriff's office will call the Civilian Liaison Officer at the JAG headquarters with a list of people for whom they have paperwork.

Then, on Thursday, the sheriff's office will send a deputy to the JAG building with the paperwork. The JAG folks will then present each person on the list to the deputy who will then serve the civil paper or make the criminal arrest. If arrested the person is cuffed and taken off post to the Pulaski County Jail to begin their legal journey on their criminal charge. If there is a breaking event, and an emergency civil paper needs to be served or a criminal arrest needs to be done immediately on post, the military will usually send MP Officers or CID Agents with the civilian officer to make the arrest or serve the paper.

And yes, this is a very brief explanation of the complex legal process flow between federal and state law and leaves out a ton of detail. If I remember correctly, the memorandum that I signed back in 2009, at the start of my second term as sheriff, was about nine or ten pages long. But by and large this system works very well on both sides of the Ft. Wood boundary line.

18 CATCHING MOONBEAMS

As a member of law enforcement, you run across subjects who aren't mentally balanced occasionally in your career. Sometimes they think they're Jesus Christ, like the previous story, and sometimes they're catching radio signals in their teeth..

Late one night, Troop I got a telephone call from a homeowner who stated a man was trying to steal his car that was parked in his front yard and that he was holding the man at shotgun point. Naturally, several of us ran hot and heavy to that location, however, I just happened to be the closest Trooper to the call.

Upon arrival, the homeowner was indeed standing on his front porch pointing a shotgun at the car. The homeowner immediately yelled at me that the suspect was still in the vehicle. The car was sitting there with all the doors standing wide open and with the interior light burning. A male subject was clearly visible in the front passenger seat. I approached the vehicle and confronted this man at gunpoint.

When the man heard my voice, he turned and looked at me, and the look on his face, immediately said crazy! So, instead of the typical police commands that would be uttered at a time like this, I asked the man what he was doing.

He looked up at me as his hands rummaged through the glove box and he said, "I am collecting moonbeams." Unfortunately that was the high point of the conversation with him for the evening.

I had considerable difficulty understanding him as he tried to explain to me that the radio signals coming through the fillings in his teeth were overpowering his brain and he was having trouble thinking. Or talking. I was able to persuade him to step out of the car and come back to my vehicle without having to resort to any type of force. He did tense up on me when I tried to put a set of handcuffs on him. But again I did not have to use force.

The subject was taken to the Pulaski County jail pending a charge of auto theft. However, I knew that charge was not going to fly. This man was going to be committed to a mental care facility. A person suffering from a mental deficiency such as this man obviously had cannot be convicted of a crime because they are not in their right mind. Dealing with these people can be very tricky.

Unfortunately, we encountered mentally challenged people fairly often and you always prayed that you would never find one that wanted to use a weapon. Even though you knew these people were not in their right mind, and had no rational understanding of what they were doing, when they pointed a weapon at you, they could kill you. As an officer who wanted to go home to his family at the end of the shift, you had no choice but to respond accordingly. This scenario becomes a tragedy for the mentally challenged person and an equally tough tragedy for the police officer. It's a no-win situation.

Postscript, the state of mental health care in Missouri is not very encouraging. During my term as the elected sheriff of Pulaski County, the state of Missouri closed a considerable number of state mental hospitals and put thousands of people who needed treatment back on the streets in our cities.

Since the Sheriff's office is the primary agency that deals with the confinement of mentally disturbed people, we found that we had been placed on a list and the primary care mental hospital for all of our customers was located in the St. Louis area 200 miles away.

This was not a realistic option for emergency mental commitments. The long drive to the facility was very taxing on both the deputy and the person being committed. Many problems came about as a result of this reduction in mental care facilities. I sincerely hope, that in the future, the state of Missouri takes steps to increase the number of mental care facilities available to the citizens of Missouri who so desperately need that care.

19 HELPING KIDS

There are a number of things that are difficult about being in law enforcement. Dealing with the mentally ill is difficult, but nothing is more difficult for the heart than cases involving children. They are definitely at the top of the list for things that will haunt you.

I do not remember when this particular case occurred. Early or mid-1970's I think. It was not a Highway Patrol case. I was called into it because some of the Waynesville City Police Officers who were on the case knew that I was a fairly decent photographer and they felt that this case was screaming for good photographic documentation. And so I was called to the emergency room of the Pulaski County Memorial Hospital. The case at hand was child abuse.

According to the people from the children's division of the state welfare office, they had been watching a family for some time and attempting to locate the two small children that they knew were part of the family. They had received reports of child abuse and they desperately wanted to check these children. They got their chance one cold January morning, when they received a report that the family vehicle was parked in front of a restaurant, in downtown Waynesville, with the two kids in the car and no grown-ups in sight.

The welfare division caseworkers basically burgled the car and stole the kids. Correction, they took emergency protective custody of two small children who were in an unheated car, in January temperatures, without adults present. They took them to the Pulaski County emergency room for a medical exam. When they undressed the five-year-old boy, they received a shock. The young lad had extensive second-degree burns in and around his genital area and upper thighs. The burns were showing iridescent colors of green, red, and pink and looked extremely nasty. The burns had most likely been caused by scalding hot water. A decision was made that photographs had to be taken and my name was brought up. So there I was to take the pictures of the young child.

The first flash picture I took of him nearly made him hysterical, and he would not cooperate with the photography process. The nurses were having trouble holding him down while I tried to take the pictures, and his constant movement made the pictures worthless. Then we heard the young lad say something about, "It burns." That's when we realized that he thought the flash from the camera was going to burn him.

The particular flash unit that I was using had an energy saving feature called the power dump, which basically meant that if an excessive flash was being used to take a particular picture, a sensor in the flash unit would detect that and would cut the power off, thus saving additional battery and enabling you to take more pictures. Utilizing that feature, I told the young lad to watch this and I held the flash unit about one inch over my arm and repeatedly triggered the flash unit multiple times. One of the nurses caught on to this scheme immediately and held out her hand and said, do that to my arm. So I triggered the flash on her arm several times.

I then gave the flash unit to the young lad and had him

press the button and repeatedly flash the unit over my hand and he got into pushing the button rather rapidly and was enjoying himself. And as a result of that, we were finally able to convince the young lad to hold out his hand and I held the flash unit directly over his hand and triggered off one flash. Problem solved.

As the young lad demolished an ice cream bar, that one of the nurses had found, I took all the pictures that were needed. If you can imagine a burned area in and around the genital section of a five-year-old boy's body, and that burned area is approximately the same size as a 12 inch pizza pan with the iridescent colors of red, green, and pink, you have a pretty good idea of what we were looking at that day. In addition to the burns, the young lad had several broken bones that had healed on their own. Healed very badly.

His little sister, who was three years old, did not have any broken bones but she had cigarette burns all over her body, including her inner genital region. Somebody had deliberately held a lit cigarette against her skin. The welfare folks got with the Sheriff's Department and the children were officially seized and taken into custody. They were then placed into a foster home and we in law enforcement went looking for mom and boyfriend.

I must confess that we kinda hoped that boyfriend would resist, when we found them, but they remained hidden quite well and it was several days before they were found. By that time, tempers had cooled slightly. On that first day in the ER, had boyfriend and mom come walking through the door, I think it would've been a race between the cops and the medics to see who could kill them first. I think us cops would have won because we had guns and the medics only had scalpels. So it's probably a good thing that they disappeared for several days.

They were both charged with two counts of assault and I am pleased to note that the boyfriend got five years on each count. The judge ordered them served consecutively, which basically made it a ten year sentence. I do not remember what the court did with mom on the criminal charge. I do, however, know that approximately one year later, I went to court in another county at the request of the state welfare office and the Pulaski County Juvenile Office. I testified in a parental revocation hearing and my photographs were entered into evidence in the hearing. As a result of the hearing, mommy lost all rights to her children. Case closed, but the pictures still make me sick to my stomach.

Postscript: This is not the type of case you want to photograph. And then to be the big scary monster who approaches the little boy and is going to burn him with the flash unit and to watch his terrified reaction to the whole process. Well, frankly, it sucks. I have a better description of the event, but my editor tells me I cannot use that language in this book.

Since this was not an MSHP case and I paid for the film and finished photographs out of my pocket, I kept a full set of these photographs in my file at home. Every year or two, I pull them out and look at them again and frankly they still make me sick.

20 THE PEDESTRIAN DEER ACCIDENT

Not all of the stories in this book are humorous, as you may have figured out, but they do paint a picture of what it's like to work in law enforcement, the Highway Patrol, and Pulaski County in particular. This story falls in the not humorous category, but is the kind of thing a state trooper can come across in his or her career.

Whenever you're given a call to respond to you never quite know what you're going to find. Very frequently the details of the call that you are given are not what you find when you get on the scene. This particular story concerns a car deer accident that I was sent to near the 161 overpass, inside the St. Robert city limits. The accident, however, had occurred on I-44, so it was ours.

The radio call had given me a description of the van involved and I quickly found the van parked on the exit ramp. As I stopped behind the van, the driver came back to me and began explaining to me that he had hit a deer on the interstate about 400 yards east of where we were standing. He said he had seen the brown flash of the deer hide, as it flew off the front hood of his car. Now, I should note that, on this particular occasion, it was a dark moonless night with a heavy cloud cover and we were dealing with a stretch of I-44 that had just been repaved, so the asphalt was very black. Or in simpler terms, it was really hard to see this night and there were no streetlights in this area.

I began jotting down the information from the license plate at the rear of the vehicle. Then I wrote down the driver's information from his license. We chatted for a moment or two and then I went to the front of the car to assess the vehicle damage.

One look at the front of the vehicle and I instinctively said, "Oh shit....you hit a pedestrian!" The driver immediately told me it was a deer. I pointed to the front of the van and told him, "Knee hit here, elbow hit here and head hit here." The driver in a sudden state of panic said, "IT WAS A DEER!"

At that point, I reached up to the driver side windshield wiper and pulled a hair from the wiper that was approximately 12 inches long. I showed it to him and told him deer hair is not that long. You hit a pedestrian, stay right here, and do not leave.

I then called for assistance from other units in the area and we began scouring the interstate looking for the pedestrian. The highway department had not yet mowed the interstate right-of-way and so the weeds were very tall. But eventually we found a black female, dressed in black clothing, lying in the weeds between the westbound lane of I-44 and the North Outer Road. She was deceased on the spot. When a van running 70 mph hits a pedestrian square front, on the interstate, you really do not want to know about the injuries suffered.

I returned to the van to fill the driver in on the situation and, when I got there, I found out that he was having chest pains, and he had previously had a heart attack. So I called an ambulance for him and we sent him to the hospital. Meanwhile, the Pulaski County Coroner was called to the scene to take possession of the body.

And thus a "routine car deer accident" came to a close.

Postscript: How to explain this one? One second, you are at the top of the tallest hill, on the roller coaster ride and things are so ho-hum. It's a car deer accident, just like the hundreds of others you have worked. And then Bang! Two seconds later, you are at the bottom of the hill, with your heart pounding and the adrenaline flooding your body, as you realize he hit a pedestrian! But in that same second from the size and depth of the impact marks on the vehicle, you already know how this case ended before you even start to search for the victim. It's an emotional one-two punch you have to experience to understand. And then to add to the experience, you will never know why the victim decided to cross over I-44 on foot. Wearing black clothing, on a black night, with no streetlights. Why?

21 HIDE THIS BEFORE THE COPS GET HERE

I frequently find myself in a position where people are asking me for stories about things that happened to me during my 32 year career with the Missouri State Highway Patrol, here in Pulaski County. And there are many deep, dark, nasty, nights full of death, violence, and destruction that I can remember. I have been known to tell many stories along those lines and people do seem to enjoy them, but I thought to myself, "What would happen if I would tell the story of one of the funniest things that ever happened to me while I was working. Would such a story be a hit?".

I'm going to make a feeble attempt at humor, so please bear with me kids, this could get a little nasty. So anyway, about 1978 or 1979, I was driving a real big, dark green Mercury Interceptor patrol car, engine size 460. Waroooom! Warooom!

This particular patrol car was equipped with the infamous solid red hot dog light bar. The light bar was visible from 2 miles away and that's before you turned it on. If you can imagine a hot dog placed across the roof of the car, you have some idea of what this solid red light bar looked like.

So there I was, working day watch out of the St. Robert Zone Office, routine patrol was the name of the game for the day. I found myself thinking that the Dixon area would be a good location to go look for various bad guys and despicable folks, so I headed for Dixon. After I had patrolled around the Dixon area for an hour or so, I came to the conclusion that there were many more bad guys up there than I had real bullets for, even allowing for all one shot hits and no misses. I decided that I probably should get out of Dixon. So there I was, minding my own business, southbound on Highway 28, near that scenic overlook known as Portuguese point.

It was a bright clear day, about 3:30pm in the afternoon, perfect visibility, no problems, and as I rounded the curve near Portuguese point, I saw the vehicle coming at me suddenly swerve to the left and run off the left side of the road, into the ditch right in front of me. Had I been a few seconds further south on the road, this would have been a very different story. The front end of the car dug into the ditch line and threw dirt, debris, and leaves high into the air and before the leaves started falling back to the ground, I was parked on the right hand shoulder facing the wreck.

Like a good professional, I remembered to turn my light bar on and the solid red hot dog lit up the surrounding countryside like a sunset. I even remembered to put my trooper boy hat on before I walked up to the vehicle. So as I approached the vehicle, I could see that there were two people in the front of the vehicle, one driver, one passenger, as is the normal routine, and I could see one passenger in the rear seat. The impact of the collision with the ditch did not appear to be severe and I suspected that there would not be any injuries in this particular wreck, but the fact that the car had swerved across the center line in front of me and then run off the road caused me to believe that there might be some fermented grape or barley juice in the immediate vicinity and that possibly, I should take a much closer look at the situation.

When you work vehicle wrecks long enough, pardon me, I mean accidents, we are supposed to call them accidents. When you work accidents long enough, you soon realize that fermented grape and or barley juice combined with pink elephants crossing the road caused quite a few wrecks in our County and just about every other County. You do realize that due diligence requires you to keep a lookout for the aforementioned fermented grape or barley juice and understand the effects that it has on unsuspecting individuals who attempt to maneuver a car down a two lane road. So, in my full professional enforcement mode, I walked up to the side of the vehicle. It was diagonally across from me in the ditch and, as I said before, I was in full uniform. I even remembered to wear my hat and, directly behind me, in broad daylight, was the big green machine, I mean patrol car, with the big red hot dog on the roof going wink, wink, wink. So, I believe that most people would recognize that the police were on the scene and in some cases, that would probably create panic.

As I walked up to the car, the female passenger in the rear seat of the car suddenly steps out of the vehicle and looks around the roadway, looks at me, looks at the patrol car behind me, looks back at me again, and then without a word she disappeared back into the car. As I stood there wondering what was going to happen next, she suddenly appeared from the vehicle again holding two very frosty cold bottles of a particular brand of fermented barley juice made in the St. Louis region of the state of Missouri in her hands.

As she stood there with these two bottles of fermented barley juice in her hand, I wondered what she was going to do with them. And then, suddenly, I got my answer because she handed the two bottles to me and said and I quote, "Quick, get rid of these before the Trooper gets here."

She then dived back into the car and, after rummaging around for a moment or so, she came back out with two more cold bottles of fermented barley juice and started to hand them to me. At that point, she suddenly let out a little shriek and said something that sounded like and I quote, "Where did you come from?"

Now, a moment ago, I was talking about my professionalism and dedication to the job and so forth, and let me just be clear that, at that particular moment, all of that went completely out the window and I busted out laughing just about as hard as I could laugh. The situation did not get any better when the driver and the front seat passenger both got out of the car and almost collapsed in the roadway dying of laughter. The poor lady standing there with the two cold bottles in her hand turned about as red as the big red hot dog on top of my patrol car and had a really confused look on her face.

I would like to say that I was very professional in investigating this accident. I went back to my car and got my accident notebook and commenced to asking all the silly questions we ask at a time like this, while gathering the details for my written motor vehicle accident report. If I said something about being professional, I lied. Every time I looked at the lady, I busted out laughing again, and every time I did manage to regain my composure, either the front seat passenger, or the driver would explode in laughter and I would find myself forced to join them. This turned out to be one of the most unprofessional wrecks I ever worked in my career. I know it was because at the end of the investigation, after we got the car pulled out of the ditch using a wrecker and they went on their way again, my ribs hurt.

It was just one of those silly situations that sometimes happen, the driver who was talking to the passenger lost control. His speed was under the speed limit and I know that, not because he told me so, but because I was watching him when he had the wreck. So, basically, the wreck was not that drastic of a situation and the driver had not been drinking any of the fermented barley juice, so there was no DWI charge. All in all, there really wasn't much of a violation, so they did not drive off with my autograph on a yellow piece of paper.

The only good thing that came out of this wreck was

the fact that I had called it into my troop radio dispatch when it happened. They knew I was on the scene of a vehicle accident, and it was kind of hard to explain to the dispatcher over the radio that the only injuries from this motor vehicle accident occurred during the extreme laughter that the occupants of the vehicle, well two of the occupants, and the investigating officer were forced to suffer during the course of the investigation. Needless to say, dispatch was not impressed with my explanation and the entire situation simply faded away into the sunset.

22 STOLEN CAR?

In police work, a lot of strange things happen and this particular story might be an example of an odd occurrence. For some strange reason, in the summer of 1970, the senior Troopers in the zone all disappeared toward Troop I for some kind of a meeting and left behind two young Troopers to take care of the zone while they were gone. And so little old me, the experienced eight month veteran of the Highway Patrol was acting as the Field Training Officer for the two-month experienced veteran of the Highway Patrol. Obviously as we patrolled about this was a recipe for disaster.

The new Trooper, who had been on the patrol approximately two months when this happened, was Trooper David B. Hart, badge 220. Dave is no longer with us, he passed away many years ago, but knowing his sense of humor, I don't think he would mind having his name in this story.

As we patrolled along Interstate 44, we found a car parked on the road shoulder with Mississippi plates. There appeared to be two people in the vehicle sound asleep. I requested a stolen check on the vehicle from Troop I and, acting as the big shot FTO officer, I asked Trooper Hart what he would do if the car came back as stolen. Trooper Hart said he would immediately run up and grab the passenger and he expected me to grab the driver and together we would get the situation secured. I told him that sounded like a good plan and he was going to make a great Trooper.

About that time, Troop I radio advised us that it was a stolen vehicle, we looked at each other in amazement for about two seconds, and then we charged the vehicle. We removed the two young, formerly soundly sleeping, males from the vehicle and handcuffed them rather smartly. We then searched the vehicle and found nothing. I went back to the radio to tell Troop I that the new Trooper nugget's had the world under control. When the Troop I radio operator responded to my radio call, his voice sounded strangled as he said, "733, I think there's been a mistake."

It turned out that the Mississippi license plate we ran had turned up nine different stolen cars, three stolen pickups, one motorcycle, and one boat. Obviously there had been a really big entry mistake of some kind. More likely a whole bunch of mistakes. Hoping to salvage the situation, we quickly copied the vehicle identification number on the Mississippi car and ran the VIN number for stolen. It came back clean.

And so Dave and I had to un-handcuff and un-arrest the two young, slightly terrified, males and we felt terrible about the screw-up. We repeatedly offered to take them down the road to a restaurant and buy them breakfast. However, the young lads had evidently had enough of the crazy young Missouri Troopers and they elected to move westbound on I-44 as soon as possible. The non-case was closed.

23 ADVENTURES IN FTO LAND

As a senior Trooper in the zone you always ran the risk of being designated as the next field training officer, FTO, for the newest rookie Trooper straight out of the Highway Patrol Academy. This assignment usually led to a lot of stress and anguish because, on day one, when you took the new rookie Trooper out into the real world where anything could happen, you were in a position where you basically knew very little about the man before that day. Surprise was usually the order of the day.

This will be a short article. Story number one involves us, my new rookie Trooper and I, responding to what had been called a burglary in progress. This particular call was in a rural section of the county, in a heavily wooded area. The female homeowner greeted us at the front door and said she could hear somebody trying to break into the back of her barn. She said she had last heard him just a minute or so before we got there.

My rookie and I approached the barn and, as we did, we heard a racket around back, so we came around the back of the barn with guns drawn and confronted .... a deer hung up in the fence right behind the barn, trying desperately to get free. We assisted the four-legged burglar in escaping from the cleverly laid trap that the homeowner had erected.

On another occasion, on the night shift, we went to an alarm sounding call. When we arrived at the residence, I took the front door and told my rookie to take the back door. The rookie Trooper promptly ran around back and jumped the fence into the backyard to advance toward the door. When he did that, two very large German shepherds, very large dogs, came out of nowhere, advancing on him, letting him know he was in the wrong backyard. The rookie Trooper promptly jumped back over the fence and came around to the front of the house and confronted me about the dogs.

No, rookie, I did not know there were two German shepherds in the backyard. Had I known, I would've warned you. I don't even want to think about the paperwork I would have to fill out if I lost my rookie in the middle of an FTO session. Yes, it was a false alarm.

Postscript: The job of an FTO was a very critical step at the start of a new Troopers career. I know that I poked humor at the FTO job in the stories before, but the actual job was deadly serious. The actions, words, and responses of the senior Trooper had a very molding and shaping effect on the new guy. Your traits became his traits in many cases. For myself, when I became an FTO, I thought of it as training a man who would be with the patrol for close to 30 years. That made it a very important job and one that had to be done right.

There was also the realization that, after the new guy was on his own solo patrol status, some dark and stormy night, when I was in deep trouble, he might be the guy coming to rescue ME. And that meant his training had damn well better have been done correctly or else I might regret skipping a few lessons with him. So I took the FTO job extremely serious.

24 HOLD UP AT DEVILS ELBOW

The days of CB radio traffic produced other situations and events in Pulaski County. One such situation involved a small mom-and-pop convenience store located just off the eastbound lane of I-44 in Devil's Elbow, Missouri. The store was owned and operated by Verl West whose CB handle was "The Piney Runt."

Piney Runt was constantly on the CB radio talking to passing truck drivers and since the store made sandwiches to order for passing motorists, it soon became a haven for tractor-trailer drivers who regularly drove through Pulaski County. With the truck drivers stopping there, the Smokey Bears stopped there as well. The store was soon a place where truckers and Smokies met in a social setting to mix and mingle. We reached the point in life where it was not unusual for an off-duty local trooper to be sitting in the store talking to the Piney Runt or a passing truck driver.

On this particular occasion, I was off-duty and was sitting in a chair behind the big potato chip rack, talking to the Piney Runt. We kept getting interrupted by the arrival of customers and Verl would have to get up and take care of their needs. I had been sitting there for about an hour and was in no hurry to go anywhere, when I looked out in the parking lot and saw a man walking toward the store with a rifle in his hands. This, of course, is the sort of thing that you wonder about, and wonder what's going to come next, especially since I did not recognize the man.

The man entered the store and immediately pointed the rifle at the Piney Runt, who was behind the front counter by the cash register, and said, "Give me the money!" The statement was rather emphatic and was made with a raised voice. The situation appeared to be serious as hell. I immediately stood up and drew my trusty 9 mm semiautomatic off-duty weapon and started to step around the potato chip rack with the front sight lining up on the guy with the rifle. Condition Red all the way around.

Suddenly, the Piney Runt began screaming at the top of his voice, "He's a friend, it's a joke, he's a friend, it's a joke!" The man with the rifle looked at him with a somewhat puzzled look on his face and then the Piney Runt pointed to me standing by the potato chip rack with my weapon leveled at him and the Piney Runt said, "Meet Trooper King."

The guy with the rifle wilted on the spot. He turned pale at the sight of my 9 mm pointed directly at him and he immediately dropped the rifle on the counter. The Piney Runt snatched the rifle up and stuck it behind the counter out of sight. Everybody took a step back at the same time and blood pressures that had been going up sharply began to spiral back down, headed toward normal.

As much as I regret to say this, I had some stern words of wisdom for the charming young man who displayed such stupidity, when he walked in the door with the rifle and pointed it at the store clerk. In fact, you could say I issued him a very severe Alpha Charlie for several minutes. And if you don't know what an ass chewing is now you do. Never a dull day in Pulaski County..

25 THE IGA BURGLARY

Many years ago in St. Robert, Missouri, the IGA supermarket stood on the edge of the city route. This market was a favorite for all of the local officers because, if you showed up around 4:30 a.m. at the back door, the Baker would invite you in and you would be surrounded by freshly cooked and freshly iced donuts. Help yourself boys. This tactic, on the part of the IGA, ensured that there were quite a few officers around their store at odd times and made them a lot harder target for thieves to crack.

One charming morning, around 2 a.m. or so, as I was driving west on the city route in St. Robert, I saw two St. Robert patrol cars coming up behind me with their red lights going. I had heard no radio traffic dispatching them to anything and that usually meant that they had been at the office when the call came in, so there had not been any radio traffic. The lead car pulled up alongside me and I could see that it was driven by St. Robert City Police Chief Hiram "Ben" Cooper.

I reached for my radio microphone to ask him what was going on and, when Ben saw the microphone, he pointed at it and shook his head no. He then gave me the follow me sign and the two cars took off westbound. I tagged along behind him. When we got to the IGA supermarket, Ben parked in front of the building by the front door and the other officer went around to the rear entrance. I stayed up front with Ben.

After a few seconds on the scene, I realized that the glass panel in the lower part of the front door to the IGA had been busted out and this, apparently, was going to be a burglary in progress call. When Ben got out of his patrol car, we met at the rear of his car and he told me that this had been called in as a burglary in progress by a passing motorist, who had evidently witnessed the guys breaking into the building. There were supposed to be at least two suspects in the building. With the building entrances covered to prevent escape, Ben got on the radio requesting assistance from the Pulaski County Sheriff's Department and I called in a couple of the other Troopers who were working that night.

Once we had a small herd of officers on scene, we entered the building to search for the suspects. As I remember the building, there was a long storage hallway on the left side of the building that ran all the way to the rear of the building. As several of us were looking in that storage side and slowly moving forward, the officer in front of me stepped on a hand and the owner squealed loudly.

The burglary suspect had rolled under the storage shelf at ground level, but there was not enough room for his entire body to fit. He had not done too badly. Two other officers had stepped completely over him without discovery.

This suspect was quickly cuffed and led out of the building. A minute or so later, another cheer was heard and suspect number two emerged from the building. During the search, we also found a portable CB radio hidden near one suspect which told us that there had been a lookout on the outside of the building, who was probably monitoring the police radio channels for any traffic related to the burglary. Or in simpler terms smart move BEN!

When the suspects were run for any possible criminal record, we found that they each had a string of burglary arrests and convictions that seemed to be a mile long. We had bagged professional burglars from the St. Louis area.

26 THE ARMED ROBBERY I MISSED

The wide and varied nature of the criminal cases we got into in the 1970's era was staggering. However, one of the consequences of our constant criminal work was the fact that we frequently developed reliable informants. Some of the Troopers had really reliable informants. This is a case were a very reliable informant had whispered in the ear of one of the supervisory officers in the zone and told him of a criminal event that would occur shortly. The armed robbery of a gas station/salvage yard.

The supervisor decided that it would be a really good idea if he put me in a wrecked car that was parked about twenty steps from the front door of this particular gas station. And there I sat in the darkness with my shotgun waiting for the robbery to occur, bored out of my mind at the inaction of the evening, yet on edge because at any second there could be heavy action. The first night nothing happened. Toward morning the supervisor picked me up and I went home to sleep.

The second night was a different story. Almost the same story, well not exactly. Around 2 a.m, the supervisor picked me up and halfway apologized for wasting my time because obviously the information from his informant was incorrect. An hour and a half later, the gas station was robbed at gunpoint by three men. Since I had nothing to do with investigating this particular crime, I had to go to the newspaper files to get the information on this one. And now for the rest of the story.

When the three guys held the place up, they destroyed the telephone in the station and a police radio scanner. Since this was also a time when a gas crisis was going on in the nation, they took the liberty of filling their car up without paying for gasoline. Brilliant criminals that they were, they forgot something very important.

When they fled the station, the gas hose was still in their tank. As they ripped the gas hose line off the gas pump, the gas hose line also ripped the rear license plate off their vehicle. And so lying right there, on the ground, in front of the officers, was a hot clue as to who committed the robbery. It was probably just a coincidence that the license plate registration came back to the same guy that the informant had said was going to rob the place?

The main suspect was quickly located and placed in the Waynesville City Jail because Pulaski County did not have a jail at this time. The new jail began operation around February of 1976. However, a short time later, two of the suspects from this armed robbery escaped from the Waynesville City Jail by digging a hole in the wall just above the door. Later that night, they stole a car in Waynesville and fled to Illinois. The car was later recovered abandoned in Illinois. The main suspect in this armed robbery was later caught and as a result of his crime spree had additional charges filed against him in Indiana and Michigan.

This one could have been a nightmare. Had the three of them held the place up while I was hidden there in the dark, I would have faced 3 to 1 odds. I had been told only one robber would hit the place. There would also have been a potential hostage inside the building. This armed robbery in progress situation could have gotten very nasty in a hurry. My only course of action would have been to surprise them and try to overpower them with the sudden shock of surprise. Disarmed and on the ground real fast. Otherwise, I could only try to contain them in the building until backup arrived.

I can still argue this one both ways. I would have been proud to be there to take enforcement action. I was also proud not to have been there, when they came out the door, because somebody would have been hurt. The hostage standing between us would have been a major problem and his chance of injury would have been quite high.

27 HE HID THE MONEY WHERE?

There is nothing quite like working as a patrol officer during the annual Fourth of July fireworks week full of booms and bangs. You're constantly looking over your shoulder to see if you're being shot at and then after a while, you reach a point where if you were being shot at, you wouldn't realize it in time to duck.

Fireworks week also brings with it a litany of things you could do without, such as the fireworks complaints, people shooting them across a highway or into somebody else's back yard. And then the kids throwing lit fireworks out the car window as they speed along. Boom!

But for me, the Fourth of July week often brought fireworks of another kind for several years running and so we will start the saga of fireworks week in the next two chapters. The first story will be that of an armed robbery that occurred at Al's liquor store on the Fort Wood spur on July 4, 1974.

The details of the case were simple, two men armed with a bolt action 7 mm Mauser rifle entered Al's liquor store shortly after dark and demanded money. The two robbers fled from the store a minute or two later with several hundred dollars in cash and jumped into a vehicle driven by a third-party. An investigation at the scene quickly determined a pretty good description on the suspect vehicle.

Later that night, Troopers and other local officers located the vehicle and we were able to take all three men into custody at a local motel. We also recovered the Mauser rifle and most of the stolen cash. Charges against the three men were quickly filed and we were headed for Circuit Court.

The circuit court trial of the third man, who was charged in connection with the armed robbery and named as the getaway driver, got rather interesting. I found myself on the witness stand, in front of the jury. I had to testify to the fact that, while searching this defendant, I recovered roughly one third of the stolen cash from this suspect. The prosecutor then asked me where I found this money.

I had the honor to look the jury right in the eyes and tell them that I recovered this money from the man's underwear where it was wrapped around his penis. If you

ever want to testify in open court, in front of a jury, try that line and see how YOU feel. Anyway, upon hearing me say that the jury's reaction was hilarious. All twelve members of the jury blinked their eyes and their mouths came open about an inch. They did that in unison.

Then in unison, all twelve members of the jury turned and stared at the defendant for about five seconds. Then again, in unison, all twelve members of the jury turned back and looked at me. It appeared, from the looks on their faces, that the trial was effectively over at that point. But the trial continued for another day and a half before the jury returned a guilty verdict.

There is also a sad postscript to this case. On November 21, 1993, Mr. Albert Holtslaw, the owner of Al's Liquor Store, was found stabbed to death in the back of his store. It appeared that Holtslaw had once again been the victim of an armed robbery and had been stabbed to death during the crime. His murder was never solved.

Since I am still a member of the Pulaski County Sheriff's Department Detective unit, I would like to say that if anyone reading this story has information that could lead to solving this case please call the department at 573-774-6196 and give his loved ones some closure.

28 THE KALAMAZOO MURDERER

The second story from Fireworks week will be the story of an arrest in a murder case that I made on July 4, 1975. Yes fireworks week wasn't very kind to me sometimes, but this case ended satisfactorily for all involved except maybe the suspect.

Once upon a time...........well actually every year that I worked for the Missouri State Highway Patrol, I kept a yearly journal of my daily activity and notes on special events that happened on any given day. When I remembered another story I could safely tell around these parts, I consulted with my box of journals. For this case, I actually remembered the year that it happened as 1975. And even better, the 1975 journal was not one of the missing books. I must confess that several years' worth of my journals have disappeared from the storage box and I have no clue what happened to them.

On July 4, 1975, I was part of a heavy Fourth of July day traffic crew and I came on duty at 9:00 a.m. According to my handy little journal, I wrote 17 traffic tickets that day for moving violations and I bagged a murder suspect wanted by the Kalamazoo Michigan Police Department.

Just a minute or so after I came on the air at 9:00 a.m.

to start my shift, Troop I radio repeated a BOLO (Be On the Look Out) message for a suspect wanted for murder. The suspect had left a St. Louis area motel right at 8:00am and was believed to be heading west on I-44. The vehicle was described as a Black/White 1975 Chevrolet with a Michigan plate. I won't give the plate number in case it hasn't been retired. The white male suspect was said to be armed and dangerous, use caution if observed.

During the next few hours, little old me and every other Trooper on duty watched I-44 westbound traffic like a hawk. Nothing happened, the suspect car just vanished. Around 1:00 p.m., being somewhat tired and thirsty, I left I-44 and started east on Mo. 17 in dear old Waynesville. About 100 yards west of what is now the Waynesville Middle School, I met a westbound 1975 Chevrolet with a white body and black roof. As it went by me, I thought it had a Michigan plate and I noted the last three numbers on the plate as matching the plate for the vehicle we were looking for.

My immediate reaction was no that can't be the car.............but as I hit my brakes, in the rear view mirror I saw the car floor it, and yes that was going to be the car! I spun through the parking lot to my left and the chase was on.

When the suspect got to Rt. T, he turned north on old time Rt. T and increased speed. My first thought here was "if you want to play chase on curvy Rt. T that I know well and you do not............well I know which curve you will wreck out on mister." I continued to close the distance and was able to confirm the plate as correct. I was behind the broadcast suspect bad guy wanted for murder.

Surprise! When we got to the top of the hill, just north of Trower Hollow, the suspect vehicle suddenly stopped in the right lane of traffic, he made no attempt to park on the road shoulder. I immediately bailed out of my patrol car, with my trusty Remington pump .12 gauge shotgun in hand, and ordered the driver to get out of the car. He complied and also raised his arms high as ordered. As he was stopping, I had just enough time to tell Troop I he was stopping as I skidded to a stop. Nothing else.

I had no intention of approaching him until my backup arrived, but the suspect got nervous looking down the barrel of my shotgun and told me, "You have nothing to fear I threw the gun away after I killed her!"

I told him to shut up and gave him his Miranda rights from memory. I asked if he understood those rights and he said yes. He then repeated his statement that you have nothing to fear.

We then entered into a long unknown period of time where chaos was the order of the day. Troop I was calling me on the radio and I was not answering. I had no intention of taking my eye off him in order to enter my car to use the radio. I was quite comfortable with the situation as it was. Troop I was calling my backup cars and they were also not answering the radio. Troop I radio was getting much louder and somewhat more frantic as the passing minutes rolled onward. Meanwhile, the suspect continued to talk.

He told me where he bought the gun and ammo, two stores, he named both and their address. He told me how he had broken in and laid in wait for the victim, in her dark garage, and shot her eleven times when she entered the garage. He told me which underpass he had thrown the gun out of his car, behind some bushes ....and he just kept on talking.

After several minutes, I knew I would never remember all of his confession, but I kept the shotgun pointed right at him and he continued to talk. And talked, and talked, but the one thing he never did tell me was why he suddenly quit running from me on Rt. T. Meanwhile, Troop I radio got even louder and much more frantic.

I should probably mention that, while all of this was going on, I had to direct traffic on Rt. T around our vehicle stop location due to the fact we had closed down the north bound lane of travel. And we were on a hillcrest just around a curve. I definitely did not need a motor vehicle accident at my murder stop scene. I got some really wild looks from passing drivers as I directed them around our stopped cars.

Finally, after one or two ice ages had advanced and receded from the Ozark landscape, a backup car arrived on scene and we cuffed the bad guy. I immediately jumped into my car and grabbed paper and pen to franticly scribble down short notes on everything I could remember him saying. I did not get it all, but it did not matter. When we got the bad guy to our local zone office, he fessed up again after a second Miranda advisement in front of more witnesses. He also waived extradition back to Michigan in court.

A few days later, two Kalamazoo Michigan Detectives flew into Ft. Wood, in a chartered light plane, and I picked them up at Forney Field. They were very happy to get copies of my written reports and his confession. As a matter of fact, they got downright excited about the purchase receipt from the gun store for one new Ruger 10/22 rifle bought with his credit card number less than 48 hours before he killed her. I had spoken to the Detectives on the telephone the day of the arrest and they had already recovered the blood stained rifle from behind the bushes under the highway overpass. Now they had proof of the purchase by the suspect without having to apply for a subpoena. Can you spell premeditation?

Then the rest of the story from the Detectives. After shooting the victim, Mr. Nice Guy had called the victim's daughter and told her she better go to her mom's house and check on mommy. The daughter got a shock to say the least because the Detectives told me he had left out a few details in his confession to me. Details like the fact that, after the victim was down on the garage floor with eleven bullet holes in her, he had reloaded and shot her ten more times. He then rammed the slender rifle barrel into one of the wounds and used the sharp and narrow front sight on the rifle to rip open her abdominal wall and expose the abdominal cavity and…..………....like I said Mr. Nice Guy.

The daughter got her revenge, though. She told the Kalamazoo Detectives that bad guy had been dating her mom for some time and she felt she understood his evil mind. She told the Detectives that he would call her the next morning and taunt her some more about killing her mother. So the Kalamazoo Detectives set up a recorder and a trace on her home phone and bingo! He called. During their talk, the daughter was able to goad him into several very nice statements that the Detectives felt would play right well in front of a Jury. They also traced the call to a specific motel in west St. Louis County where responding officers from that jurisdiction arrived on scene just minutes after he had left. That's when the BOLO was broadcast statewide.

I loaded up the two detectives and Mr. Nice Guy in my patrol car and drove to Forney Field, where special arrangements had been made for the prisoner transfer. I drove him right to the waiting aircraft on a taxiway just off the main runway. Mr. Nice Guy then went bye-bye up into the air.

The following year, on May 11, 1976, while driving to Kalamazoo for a second scheduled court appearance, the trial had been continued on the first try, as I was halfway across Illinois Troop C radio at St. Louis was able to get a message to me over the radio that he had entered a guilty plea to murder second that morning. The case was now officially over.

There was kind of a postscript to this case. I was traveling to Kalamazoo with another Trooper who had heard the man's confession and we had both been subpoenaed to court. We had borrowed our lieutenant's unmarked patrol car and were cruising along in the middle of Illinois and bored out of our minds. The other Trooper was driving and he was also trying to stir things up on CB channel 19 with the truck drivers.

This went well for a while until, "Traveling Joe", asked for another update on Smokies. Almost immediately a truck driver responded with the question, "What did you say your handle was again?" When my partner said "Traveling Joe", the truck driver immediately came back with, "Hey I know that voice that's Dudley Do-Right from down around Waynesville." So I took the CB mike and said something on the air, and the same truck driver immediately came back with, "Hey it's the Green Stamp Collector what are you guys doing up here?"

So much for attempting to sneak across Illinois incognito in the lieutenant's completely unmarked car. We were caught cold and the driver had both of our CB handles correct, so we dropped into the convoy that he was running with and chitchatted with them for quite a few more miles until we got the recall notice over the patrol radio.

29 BE CAREFUL WHO YOU RIDE WITH

The third story from fireworks week will be another case of armed robbery arrests that occurred on July 6, 1976. My memory of this case is vague as to the small details and the newspaper morgue search came up empty. All my yearly journal had to say was armed robbery arrests on this date. No details. This one started with a dispatch message as to an armed robbery that had occurred in either Greene or Webster County. The suspects were thought to be headed east in a specific color van. A specific time element of travel was also given.

By this time, I had been on the road long enough to develop my own little rule of thumb. Whatever time element was given in the message, such as he left 30 minutes ago which would be about 40 miles worth of travel double it immediately to 80 miles of travel and act accordingly. In this case, doubling the time meant they would be right on top of me at any minute or maybe would have already passed me in the last few minutes. So I swung over to the east lane of I-44 and parked on the road shoulder.

The third vehicle to pass by was a van of a color close enough to the described color of the getaway van that it had to be checked. I made the stop and was quickly backed up by two other Troopers. Almost immediately, the three men in the van started looking good as suspects. Two of the men were brothers who did not like cops and were defiant. The third guy was different. Shy, scared and bashful. Within a matter of a few minutes, we developed probable cause to arrest the three for the armed robbery.

Three bad guys and three Troopers. We each grabbed one guy and started for the jail. I grabbed the different acting fellow. This man was clearly rattled by the armed robbery charge and I sensed he wanted to talk. I spent the next 45 minutes trying to get him to open up.

Finally he said the magic words, "What would happen if a guy was hitching a ride and the people in that car did a robbery? Would he also be guilty?"

We discussed that point for a minute or two and he then told me he had been in the van when the other two guys had committed the robbery. He gave me some background information on his hitchhiking adventures in Missouri and told me a Missouri Trooper had driven past him very slowly about an hour before the robbery occurred. It took about an hour to locate the Troop D Springfield Trooper who had driven by him on I-44, but when we did that, the Trooper described our guy down to the smallest detail. Case closed.

30 THE FLUSH DOCTOR

The next story will be a tale of a pursuit involving a medical doctor who was high on prescription pills. Bad guys come in all shapes and sizes, as well as all walks of life. Drugs can affect just about anyone and this guy is a prime example.

In order to understand the case correctly, I'm going to have to first give you a little lesson in moving radar operation and theory. A radar unit sends out a radio wavelength frequency that goes out several hundred to several thousand feet until it hits an object and then bounces back to the radar unit. The software processing chips inside the unit can then tell you how fast the moving vehicle is coming at you.

In addition to the visual sighting of the mile-per-hour display on the radar unit, there is a second feature built into most radar units and that is the audio Doppler tracking system. The most common analogy here is, if you're standing at a train station and hear the train coming into the station it gets louder, louder, louder, and then suddenly as it passes you by there's a definite change in tone and pitch of the train noise. A radar unit works in much the same way and, with a little practice, you can visually and with audio track your violator from the second you check him all the way down to when he passes your vehicle in the other lane of traffic.

This system also works well on the high-speed violator who is running with the radar detector on his dash and feels invincible. If you run with your radar off and wait until he will be the next car to enter the radar beam you can turn it on and lock him in at top speed in about two seconds. You then get to watch his front end dip as he brakes hard and watch the MPH display drop sharply and listen to a definite change in the tone of the pitch on the audio tracking feature. Bottom line, you checked the correct car.

So, on this particular evening, shift traffic on I-44 was scarce late at night. It was approaching midnight and there simply were not any cars out there. For some reason, as I started west from the Buckhorn overpass, I had my radar unit turned on and the unit suddenly picked up a car coming at me at 70 miles an hour on the visual screen and I was also able to track the vehicle with the audio feature. The only problem was that I couldn't see any car in the eastbound lane.

Both signal indicators continued to get stronger and stronger indicating a car coming right at me and I still could not see a car. And then, all of a sudden, I realized as the pitch on the radar changed completely, that a car had just passed me in the eastbound lane running 70 miles an hour without any lights on at midnight. A bonanza of moving violations and probably a drunk the boot!

I jumped the median and went after the car. When I got in behind the car, I turned my red lights on and instead of stopping, he turned his lights on and boosted his speed to close to 100 mph. The chase went eastbound from Buckhorn headed toward St. Robert.

The vehicle was weaving all over the roadway and it clearly was an intoxicated driver. When the driver got to the Fort Wood overpass, he took the exit ramp and entered the I-44 spur heading toward Fort Leonard Wood. He ran the red light at the Ramada intersection. By this time, several other patrol cars were with me and we were all chasing him down the spur. When he got to the next set of traffic lights, the light was red, so he stopped his vehicle as required. One of the other Troopers in the chase jumped out of his car and ran up to the guy's vehicle. Just as he got his hands on the driver side door of the suspect vehicle, the light turned green and the bad guy took off southbound again. A few hundred yards later, we basically crowded him off the road into the ditch. He was pulled from the vehicle and handcuffed immediately by approximately five officers.

The driver turned out to be a Lt. Col. Doctor in US Army Medical Corps and he was higher than a kite on prescription pills. We took him to the Pulaski County Jail and gave him a room for the night while I proceeded to write a large number of moving citations. A short time later, two CID officers showed up and inquired as to the status of the driver and when I explained the situation to them, one of them said you can't arrest a field grade officer. I told him well I've already done it and he's in the jail.

The CID officers indicated that they would have to take custody of him immediately. I told them they were welcome to the guy because we could always get him with a warrant and his medical problem would now be their medical problem.

I invited them into the back of the jail and took them to the cell were the good doctor was sitting and invited them to look in the door window. The good doctor was sitting on top of the water tank of the commode and had his feet, shoes, and socks all in the bowl of the toilet and he was repeatedly flushing the toilet.

I assume he wanted to get some mud off of his shoes. He was also laughing while doing this like a semi-daemonic individual. The agents watched this scene for a moment or two, said something about consulting with a higher authority, and left the building at a high rate of speed.

About one week later, I was advised that the good doctor had resigned from the army. Case closed.

The Colonel looks a bit flushed at the moment.

31 THE MP CHASE

The presence of the United States Army base of Fort Leonard Wood in Pulaski County has led to many situations where local troopers were called to assist the military in some fashion. This particular story concerns a chase, MP Officers in pursuit of the vehicle hauling stolen government property..

During the evening shift of February 28, 1982, Zone 4 Troopers were suddenly notified by Troop I radio that military police officers were in a vehicle pursuit on Highway 17 south in Pulaski County. The chase had actually come off base in Laclede County near the Cannon Range Road, but by the time we were notified, the northbound vehicle was already inside Pulaski County.

I ran code 3 south on Highway 17 until I met the pursuit and, at that point, I swung around and got in behind the pursuit. The MP Officers' vehicle immediately pulled over and let me take the lead position. I soon discovered that this was not much of a pursuit. The truck in front of me was so heavily loaded in the truck bed that if they got above 38 miles an hour or so the front wheels of the truck came off the road pavement and they were unable to steer the vehicle. So definitely a low speed pursuit, actually more properly, a failure to stop on command situation. But at 38 miles an hour, I decided I did not need the siren to alert other drivers. This would also have been a great time to munch a snack, if only I would have had one with me. Maybe a nap.......

After a mile or two of my most boring pursuit ever, with me behind the vehicle, the suspects decided to pull over and stop. The MP Officers swarmed the vehicle and had the two men in cuffs in nothing flat. Meanwhile, a second Trooper had joined me in the chase. As we looked over the situation, it was obvious that the truck in question was very heavily overloaded and violated all of Missouri's weight regulations for transportation of materials on the Missouri highways. As required by statute, I seized the vehicle until the weight problem could be corrected. Meanwhile the MPs hauled the bad guys off back to post.

The men in custody were found to be connected to a local salvage yard that was on the Fort Wood spur at that time. Unknown to us, the Army CID unit had been investigating this particular salvage yard for some time and had sent in undercover officers to attempt to purchase stolen items. The federal officers were in the process of putting together a search warrant application for the salvage yard when the chase occurred, giving them several more paragraphs of information to use in their application for the federal search warrant.

While doing some research for this particular story, I recently learned that one of the key factors in the granting of the search warrant for the salvage yard was the presence of stolen military equipment. One of the major problems in getting a search warrant for military property is that there is so much military property available in the world of the surplus dealers that proving such property is stolen becomes rather difficult. In this case, the undercover officer had noticed rocket launchers laying on the ground and had obtained the serial numbers off these launchers.

The rocket launchers turned out to belong to an F-14

fighter aircraft out of Whiteman Air Force Base. The rocket launcher units had been stolen off of an aircraft and they were a brand-new item in the military inventory. None of these rocket launchers had ever been released into the world of the surplus dealerships. And so, the search warrant was granted and federal officers swarmed the salvage yard for several days running.

During the search of the salvage yard, the federal officers managed to solve a local mystery. Sometime back a combat engineer unit on Fort Leonard Wood had erected a 65 foot bridge on a training area site and had secured work hours for the weekend at 5 o'clock on Friday. The engineers intended to come back Monday morning and practice taking down the bridge. However, when they returned to the training area Monday morning, the bridge was gone. No clues were developed as to where it went or how it disappeared. During the search of the salvage yard, the manufacturer's identification plate for this particular bridge was discovered in a 5 gallon bucket of oily water that contained miscellaneous metal pieces. Mystery solved.

I also learned during my research that there were quite a few very large specialized tools located in the thirty plus acre salvage yard and the CID agents had requested assistance from an engineer Sergeant to come to the scene and identify some of these tools as to their purpose and usage. One of the officers assisting in the search began questioning the Sergeant as to exactly how do you identify these tools as government property. The Sergeant told him that one thing we do is we etch our Social Security numbers on the tools.

The Sergeant went on to say, "For example here's a tool just like one that was stolen from my unit and as you can see here is the Social Security number and.............
...Holy smoke this is my stolen tool!"

I was later told, that during the federal court process, there was a suppression hearing for the evidence obtained from the truck that had been involved in the pursuit. The defense contention was that federal officers had illegally seized the truck and its contents and therefore the contents were the fruit of the poisonous tree and were not admissible in court. I was told that the federal judge ruled that the Trooper had seized the truck for a weight violation pursuant to a requirement of Missouri law and therefore the stolen parts in the truck bed were admissible. At the conclusion of the federal court hearings, several people went to the federal penitentiary because of this case.

The story has a postscript. On April 9, 1982, the Fort Leonard Wood Provost Marshal, Lt. Col. Boyd R. Messinger, sent a letter of commendation to the Superintendent of the Missouri State Highway Patrol commending myself and the other trooper involved in the vehicle stop, Trooper Ralph E. Roark for our efforts in assisting the military with the pursuit and the case. In his letter Lt. Col. Messinger said, "Had it not been for the quick response and the precise action of these two fine officers, this case may never have been resolved."

Lt. Col. Messinger went on to say that the further investigation in this case led to the recovery of civilian and government properties in excess of $100,000.00. But they did not recover the bridge. It was most likely cut up and sold as high grade scrap metal.

And there is a second postscript to this case. Several weeks after the chase had occurred, during one of our conferences concerning this case, I met again with the two young MP Officers who had been involved in the pursuit. They both proudly showed me the boxed commendation medals that they had received for their actions during the pursuit from the United States Army. Ralph and I did not get a medal.

32 THE MACE FLASHLIGHT

During my career with the Highway Patrol, I was never bashful about spending my own money for items that looked like they might make my workload a little easier. At one time, I came across an advertisement for a new flashlight that had a canister of mace built into the flashlight. The basic concept was that as you had your flashlight pointed directly at the party if they did something stupid, like take a swing at you with their fist, all you had to do was shove the button forward and the Mace would squirt directly into their eyes. A beautiful concept. The flashlight had a safety feature sort of like the safety switch on a weapon that had to be thrown to the off position before you could slide the lever forward to spray the Mace. And so I purchased this nifty little package.

I used it for several years and never once had to spray a combative suspect with the Mace. But the flashlight was a major part of an event that occurred at Troop I headquarters that solidified my name into the annals of infamy at Troop I headquarters.

One of the jobs of the radio division of the Highway

Patrol is to fix and repair the radios in the patrol cars when they are out of service. For the most part, the wiring harness that helps to control the radio is located underneath the dashboard of the vehicle. The wires are located in a position where, if you have to work on them for a period of time, it can get very uncomfortable. However, one Troop I radio operator had solved the mystery of how to make these repairs in relative comfort.

This operator put his back and shoulders on the floor of the vehicle and with his head directly under the dashboard. This position also put his rear end on the car seat with his legs over the back of the seat. This was a fairly awkward, but comfortable position from which he could work on the wires underneath the dashboard for a long period of time.

Unfortunately, on this particular date in infamy, the radio operator working on my patrol car's radio, who was in that awkward position, needed a flashlight. The operator felt around on my front seat and found a flashlight, my trusty Mace flashlight. He somehow threw the gun safety switch into the off position and he sprayed Mace up under the dashboard. The Mace came dripping down onto his face. The radio operator exited my patrol car immediately from his very awkward position to the sound of tearing wires and general mayhem underneath my dashboard.

Fortunately, I was not present to receive his wrath at this disturbing event. In fact, if I remember correctly, it was several days before he caught up with me and expressed his displeasure at my equipment. And from that day forward, whenever he was going to work on my car, he demanded to know what exactly was in it and where was it and what did it do.

He also made sure that everybody he knew heard about this story and the story became firmly entrenched in the annals of Troop I infamy.

33 HUNTING RABBITS IN BALL GOWNS

Early in my career with the Highway Patrol, I went through a phase where I wanted to know how other officers and agencies worked. As a result, on my days off, I would ride a shift with municipal officers, with County deputies, and with the game wardens. As a result, when some case came up involving any of these different agencies of law enforcement, I would be better informed and better able to take effective action. I think I'm going to have to admit that the most fascinating of the three were the duties of the game wardens.

These officers had a very different approach to patrol and enforcement actions than everybody else did. And even though we frequently referred to them as the "skunk Sheriff," and they lovingly called us the "taillight detectives," both of our agencies usually got along quite well. We were able to work several things to our mutual advantage.

During the fall deer hunting season, we were known to set up spot-checks on Highway 17 South and, as a result, we would stop a lot of hunters, frequently with a deer strapped on their car, and we would be checking for violations of the vehicle code. The game wardens who would be with us would check for violations of the wildlife code. We frequently would find a man with an out-of-state driver's license, but who was in possession of a deer on a resident deer hunting license. Usually, this meant he was wrong for one of us.

As a guy who liked to hunt, I found it to be repulsive when, during a ride along with the game wardens, they would point out the carcass of a very large deer that had been shot out of season in the middle of a field. The carcasses were usually deer with the horns removed from their heads. The entire deer would be lying there, just going to waste because somebody wanted the horns and most likely shot the deer with the use of an artificial light in the middle of the night. I personally did not regard that as hunting. I thought of it more as stealing; stealing from those of us sportsmen who were willing to play by the rules, when in pursuit of a trophy deer.

As a result of exposure to violations like this, I took careful note of one statute in the Missouri game code which basically stated that it was the duty of all peace officers in the state of Missouri to diligently enforce the provisions of the wildlife code. Now, as a practical matter, I could not go play game warden all the time simply because my patrol duties would not let up long enough in order to have the time to do a little wildlife protection work. However, every once in a while, you got a chance to enforce the wildlife code.

There was one nice, crisp, fall night that I recall, prior to the start of deer season, when I was down toward the end of Highway H hoping to find a spot-lighter in action. I decided to cross over the Roubidoux River and move closer to the Laquey side of the county. We had recently had high water on the Roubidoux and, as I got to the crossing, I noted the presence of a new sandbar that was resting on rocks so I drove across. Correction, I attempted to drive across it because about 15 feet into the forward motion my car quit moving and my rear tires began to spin.

I opened the door of my patrol car to see what the problem was and, when I did that, the bottom edge of my driver-side door scraped up a mound of sand as it opened. Or in simpler terms, my car had sunk all the way to the frame of the car in the sand. Which was a whole lot deeper than I had thought. There was only one thing to do and I did it gracefully. I called Troop I on the radio and said send me a wrecker.

Sometime later, my good friend Danny Fry arrived on the scene with his wrecker to assist me. Now, I would like to be able to say that Danny promptly assisted me, but that would be a little incorrect. Danny first had to spend several minutes recovering from laughter before he could do his wrecker man duty. But he eventually got me out of the sandbar and back on the road. Thank you Danny.

On another night shift that I can remember, during one of our great floods here in Pulaski County, where I-44 travel was cut off at both the Gasconade River in Laclede County, for east bound traffic, and at the Gasconade River in Phelps County, for west bound traffic. On this particular night, I drove east on the interstate toward Route J. I'm not sure why I did this because I did not see a single car east of the Missouri 28 overpass. When I arrived Route J and got to the top of the ramp, I found a local MODOT truck and its crew sitting there in the dark waiting for a call. So I stopped to socialize for a few minutes.

After several minutes of conversation, we were suddenly startled by the sound of a gunshot just a few hundred yards away. After walking around the MODOT truck, we saw that on the westbound North Outer Road, going west from the J overpass, there was a car sitting on the gravel road. The occupants of the car were shining a spotlight across the field and had just fired a shot. Can you say game violations?

As this vehicle drove westbound, the occupants continued to shine the light over the road ditch and the edge line of the trees. While they were doing that, I moved into a blocking position at the end of the road just inside Pulaski County. When the car came back a few minutes later, I made the stop at shotgun point and told them to get out of the vehicle. Although I suspected this is probably going to be a wildlife spotlight violation, we had recently had some cattle shot and butchered in the middle of the night, so just in case that was what they were doing, I intended to give the occupants their Miranda warnings.

As the occupants of the vehicle came out of the vehicle, I found that I had five people in front of me. Three white males dressed in blue jeans and flannel shirts, more casual or even rough clothing wear, if you will. Then I had two ladies in long flowing evening dresses, with jewelry and high heels, straight from a formal ball somewhere. This was quite the contrast.

The five individuals acknowledged their Miranda rights, that I gave them verbally, and, when I asked them if they were shooting cattle, one of them said, "No, we are after rabbits." Rabbits were in season, but they could not be taken with the aid of an artificial light or from a car on a roadway. I pretty well figured that we had a game violation. Upon looking in the vehicle, I found three long guns and two freshly bullet riddled bunny rabbits bleeding all over the back floorboard and one sneaky little .25 semiautomatic pistol underneath the front seat.

I told Troop I to find me a game warden and get them out here, they had some business. And Troop I called the wardens in both Phelps and Pulaski County with no response. Since I had detained these people for several minutes at this point and no game wardens were forthcoming, I decided that I was going to have to handle this one myself. Nine uniform traffic citations, which at the time could double for a misdemeanor complaint, were written on the spot and the subjects were taken down to the Pulaski County Jail to post bond.

They were a little upset over the total number of citations I had written and one of them made the remark that he would see me in court, at which time I reminded him that the .25 semiautomatic underneath the front seat was not a misdemeanor, it was a felony. And if I had to go to court, I might as well make it worth my time. There was a sudden change of attitude and the individuals pled guilty to all charges, signed the backs of their citations, paid their fines and left. Case closed.

Postscript: I do not know why the ladies were in long evening dresses and chasing rabbits. They did not say but I did hear one make a comment to the other about a regimental ball she would never forget. So I suspect a formal military function had been held earlier that evening.

34 NEVER MESS WITH A POLICE DOG... EVER

A very simple fact of life, that many people do not understand, is that crooks need cars. They haul stolen goods and drugs in cars and they use cars to drive to or away from the scene of their crime. This usage of cars for criminal purposes also has a weak point. Law enforcement officers are well aware of the fact that bad guys are using cars in the commission of their crimes and, therefore, law enforcement officers are constantly on the lookout for those subtle clues that will tell you criminal mischief is being committed right in front of you.

The press has always had an interest in what they called the criminal interdiction process, but the reality is every time an officer makes a stop of a motor vehicle, he is looking beyond the stop to see what else might be going on that people are trying to hide. Thus, a simple stop for a missing front license plate can lead to bigger things. In Pulaski County, in the early 1970's, Trooper Dave Hart made such a stop for a missing license plate and, when he found a credit card receipt in the car in the name of a prominent local individual, it led to the smashing of a burglary ring and the clearance of probably forty or so burglaries in the area.

However, our story for this chapter is a drug case. I cannot remember what year this happened, but here is the basic story. While on routine patrol in the afternoon, Troop I radio suddenly began a series of radio conversations between Troop I and officers in the Lebanon area. The upshot of it was during a traffic stop officers had detected the presence of drugs in an out-of-state vehicle and that Illinois vehicle was now fleeing from the officers headed eastbound toward Pulaski County. The pursuing officers wanted units to take up a position on the off ramps at all overpasses that the chase was approaching to prevent the suspect from getting off of the interstate.

I immediately raced for the Buckhorn overpass. As I made a left turn to cross over the interstate, I lost the race as the suspect vehicle came to the top of the ramp and blew through the stop sign at about 70 miles an hour right in front of me. He then went right back down to the eastbound lane of I-44. The chase continued into St. Robert where, at a point just east of the Fort Wood overpass, the suspect drove off of I-44 across the right hand median onto the South Outer Road, better known as Rt. Z, in St. Robert. When he got to the Mo. 28 overpass on Route Z, he turned right and went down to the interstate once again headed east.

I should also mention that, while this chase was in progress, several large sacks flew from the van into the median and onto the road shoulders. Troopers at the tail end of the chase had already picked up several of these bags and advised us over the radio that they contained large amounts of marijuana.

We were chasing a drug mule.

I should probably also mention that several of these large sacks, which flew from the vehicle, landed in locations where we sent officers to retrieve the bundles, and the bundles were never found. We suspected some Good Samaritan passing by had picked up the bundles and had decided to dispose of it in their own special fashion.

By this time, the chase involved several police departments and the Highway Patrol. Since it was continuing eastbound, Troopers from Phelps County had moved over into Pulaski County to get into a better position to join the chase. As we came down the long hill headed toward the big Piney River Bridge, one of the Rolla zone troopers set up a spike strip on I-44 just east of the bridge. The suspect vehicle struck the spike strip squarely, throwing it into the air and off to one side of the road. All of the pursuing officers had to maneuver quickly to avoid the spike strip. Within a half a mile, the suspect vehicle skidded out of control onto the right road shoulder and partially off of the road.

Unfortunately, there was a large amount of eastbound traffic at the time and these cars did not know which way to go, so we ended up with the several very near misses on traffic crashes at this point. I personally had to take to the median to avoid a tractor-trailer and I ended up parked in the median right across the road from where the suspect vehicle had stopped. A second patrol car barely stopped short of my bumper.

I immediately ran across the road with my shotgun in hand and was able to catch up to one of the fleeing suspects and when he tripped and fell, I landed on him. I rolled the suspect over onto his face moved his hands to the rear of his back. As I was starting to apply the handcuffs to his wrist, the situation changed completely.

A fur missile belonging to the Lebanon City Police Department, usually referred to as a police dog, slid his drooling wide-open muzzle into the situation right alongside my hand that I had clamped down on the suspects arm. As the dog's teeth clamped down on the suspects arm the dog's attitude made it quite plain that this was his lunch and I should probably leave his lunch alone.

Now! This is why you never, ever, mess with a police dog. They mean business.

I immediately backed away from the suspect. The dog's handler approached and was able to pull the dog off the suspect so I went back in and handcuffed the guy. Three suspects had run from the van. We now had one in custody and a moment or two later, we had a second one in custody. However, suspect number three was much more slippery. He managed to evade our mini-manhunt that lasted for several hours in the Devil's Elbow area and he disappeared completely. Fortunately, we had been able to identify him and we had warrants outstanding for his arrest within a day or so after the incident occurred. Unfortunately, the authorities in the Chicago, Illinois, area were never able to locate him.

Approximately one year later, we were notified that the DEA and FBI had made the arrest on the suspect. We later got the rest of the story. It seems that the sneaky feds had learned that the suspect was on a cruise ship in the Caribbean. When the ship returned to its Florida port and our suspect came walking down the gangway to depart the ship, the federal officers pounced on him from both sides and had taken him into custody. Case closed.

35 WHY I'LL NEVER OWN A MOTORCYCLE

As Troopers, we are often dispatched to a motor vehicle accident that involves a motorcycle. Unfortunately, the majority of these wrecks are serious situations that can have lifetime consequences for the operator of the motorcycle. For the most part, motorcycle stories are stories that should be avoided in a book like this, if you're trying to do a little humor. There usually is very little humor in a motorcycle accident.

However, once upon a time, a friend of mine traveling on I-44 had a mechanical problem on his motorcycle go boom and he suddenly found himself skidding down the interstate on his back at probably at least 55-60 miles an hour. Naturally, the friction from the pavement caused some abrasion to his clothing. It cut right through the leather jacket he was wearing, the shirt and T-shirt he was wearing and about the first three layers of skin on his back. His entire back was beet red and oozing blood here and there and really looked like a sorry painful mess.

I gave him a ride to the Pulaski County Memorial Hospital emergency room in my patrol car. His morale was down so low that I thought I probably should stay with him for a few minutes. Since he was unable to lay on his back on the ER table, he sat facing me moaning about the perils of driving a motorcycle.

An emergency room nurse walked into the room holding what appeared to be a can of Mercurochrome antiseptic spray and she proceeded to tell him, "I'm sorry, but I'm going to have to spray your back to make sure the wounds on your back do not get infected. This is going to hurt. Are you ready?"

She began to spray back and forth, from side to side, until his entire back was painted red. And his eyes were watering. My friend did not scream or cry, but he wanted to. Watching his face as he struggled to control himself from the burning pain on his back, I made up my mind that I would never buy a motorcycle in my life. So far I have kept that vow.

And now a special word to my friend, you didn't think I would include this story in the book so surprise! This was your story and, as I promised, I did not use your name. You can hit me the next time you see me.

For those of you young folks who have never heard of Mercurochrome antiseptic spray, it was banned by the FDA in the U. S. back in 1998. For you old timers, who miss this stinging burning spray, the reason the FDA banned the sale of Mercurochrome, which is generically known as merbromin, was because it was, "not generally recognized as safe and effective." The compound also contains large amounts of mercury, which is a known hazard to health. The FDA banned the sale of the stuff across state lines which pretty much killed the product.

36 STOLEN NATIONAL GUARD TRUCK

The next story is a tale of adventure and excitement in which I was but one of many troopers involved in this particular chase along with a whole bunch of city officers. Before I tell the story, I probably need to say a couple of things about the patrol's radio system in 1982, particularly around November 23, 1982. Whenever Troop I called a car, they operated on a specific radio frequency. When the trooper replied to their message, he operated on a specific radio frequency. These frequencies were not the same. The problem came with the so-called car to car frequency, usually referred to as the two-way frequency, which used the same frequency as troop headquarters. This usually meant that on two-way traffic between troopers you were limited to 30 miles or so for reliable reception and if troop headquarters came on the air while you were talking to the other trooper, you got to repeat your message.

On this particular date in history, I was monitoring the radio frequency quite closely and I thought I heard the Lebanon zone troopers making arrangements on the two-way channel for a quick coffee stop. About that time,

Troop I radio put out a broadcast on a vehicle, described as a National Guard pickup truck, which had just left a gas station near Phillipsburg, Missouri, and had failed to pay for sixteen dollars' worth of gasoline.

A few minutes later, I heard one of Lebanon zone cars, who was enroute for coffee, tell somebody else on the two-way radio frequency that he had just spotted the National Guard pickup eastbound at Lebanon. It sounded like the trooper said he would make a stop on the vehicle real quick and send the guy back to Phillipsburg to pay for the gas. Then there was silence for several minutes on the radio.

Troop I radio suddenly came on the air with "rush traffic" for the Waynesville zone troopers. Now, in the patrol world, any time somebody was on the radio and used the phrase "rush traffic", it usually meant all Hell was about to break loose. And so it was on this occasion. Troop I radio told us that Lebanon zone Troopers, and Lebanon City Police Officers, were in pursuit of the National Guard pickup headed eastbound. The National Guard pickup had already rammed and seriously damaged one Highway Patrol car and one Lebanon City Police car.

Between Lebanon and the Missouri Highway 7 overpass in Pulaski County, three separate attempts were made by Troopers to shoot out the tires on the vehicle as it passed by them. We did not have tire spike strips in the old days, which would have been the early 70's. I was car number three to attempt the shot. In my case, the driver had already been shot at twice and he was a quick learner. As soon as he saw me on the shoulder with my shotgun, he aimed the pickup truck directly at me running 80 plus miles an hour. I quickly determined that discretion overrode valor in this particular incident. As I retreated from the roadway, I fired one round of buckshot toward the vehicle. I may have hit a Crow flying over the scene because I surely did not hit the truck. But the shot caused the driver to swerve back away from me so I think I won that round.

At the Missouri 7 overpass, the vehicle took the exit ramp and made a left turn and the chase headed toward Richland, Missouri. At this point, nobody was ahead of the vehicle except the waiting Richland City Police Officers. When the vehicle got into Richland one of their officers also fired at the vehicle with a shotgun. Once inside the city of Richland the National Guard pickup took a right turn off of Highway 7 and headed down the road leading toward the Richland City Airport.

Following my attempted shot on I-44 at the National Guard pickup, I had to run back to my patrol car and, as such, I ended up toward the tail end of the chase. As the chase entered Richland, one of the other Troopers reported on two-way frequency that the truck had turned off Highway 7 onto the road heading toward the Richland City Airport. I spun around off the chase and headed for Highway 133 and the other end of the road going to the Richland City Airfield. My intention was to set up a blocking position on this road that he could not get through since it was a narrow county gravel road.

However, it did not quite work out that way. About halfway down the road, heading toward my intersection at Highway 133, the National Guard pickup suddenly made a left turn off the gravel road. He drove through a fence and went up over a hill behind a residence. Since I was on the other end of the road, I missed this particular part of the action. I was later told that two patrol cars followed him up over the hill and stayed with him.

A short time later, the National Guard pickup came back down the hill, punched through the fence again, crossed over the gravel road, and punched through the fence on the other side of the gravel road. Unfortunately for him, the ditch on that side of the road was deeper and he damaged the transmission on the vehicle. As a result, he coasted to a stop about 50 yards from the fence in a wide open field. Several buckshot rounds then impacted the vehicle and may have led to his hasty decision to waive his hands outside of the vehicle in a surrender attempt.

The subject driving the vehicle was taken into custody and, by this point in the chase, to nobody's particular surprise, it was determined that he was not a member of the Missouri National Guard. The follow-up investigation revealed that the Missouri National Guard pickup truck had been stolen from a location in Springfield, Missouri, and the young lad driving it was evidently heading home to Indiana.

The suspect was charged in Laclede County court with first-degree assault, resisting arrest, and stealing and he was held in Laclede County jail in lieu of a $50,000 bond on each of the felony charges and a $2000 bond on the misdemeanor stealing of gasoline charge. He was also charged with driving without a license, excessive speed, and failure to drive in a single lane.

In this particular case, it was a minor miracle that nobody, including the seventeen-year-old driver of the stolen National Guard pickup, was injured. We surely had enough chances for somebody to get hurt in this one. I can tell you from personal experience that when a large National Guard pickup truck is aimed directly at you, running 80 plus miles an hour, and the guy is not slowing down, it can get kind of scary. Real quick.

Postscript: The next day the damaged National Guard truck was stored in the parking lot in front of the Richland City Police Department building. The truck had quite a few holes in its hide made by buckshot projectiles and it also had four flat tires. The photograph of the truck in the newspaper made it look very sad and lonely.

37 THE PATROLMAN VS. THE CIGARETTE MAN

Sometimes, some stories are just too good to keep to yourself. As law enforcement officers, we have to be able to laugh at ourselves. I know I have several times in this book. We also have to laugh at each other when we get the chance. And so, now, I bring you a tale of danger and a case of mistaken identity..

It was a dark and stormy night..........suddenly a shot rang out...........and the dog was in danger........Wait a second, that's the wrong story. But this story did take place on a dark night in St. Robert, Missouri. About 1980, just after the start of the New Year, is when our story took place. Two of St. Robert's finest patrolmen were on duty, seeking out bad guys, in the dark of the night. One Patrolman was sort of a young squirt at the police game and was still learning the ropes when suddenly.........

He drove past a sporting goods store on the city route and out of the corner of his tired young eye, he saw a man move in a closed for the evening store. Burglary in progress! The young Patrolman wisely disregarded the "One Ranger one riot approach", and, instead of going in solo, he called for help. Since it was an otherwise dull night shift, he was quickly joined by the other St. Robert Officer on duty. Several Troopers, one or two Deputy Sheriffs and we might have even had a Waynesville City Officer on the scene before this one was over. The hard part was getting the store owner out of bed and on scene with the key to the door.

Once the owner opened the front door, the search, with pointed shotguns, began in earnest. One by one we cleared the rooms in the store until the only room left was the one where the young patrolman saw the man moving around.

We slammed into that room in force and to shouts of "Don't Move!! And "Freeze!!" backed by aimed shotguns, we effectively took the six foot tall cardboard cutout of a famous Cigarette smoking man, wearing a cowboy hat into custody. The young Patrolman explained several times to all of us on scene that he did clearly see the man move before we entered the store.

His backup officer from St. Robert agreed with him. The young Patrolman also proudly stated that when he told the man to "Freeze!!" the man did not move. Let's just say the rest of us were somewhat amused by his assertion that Cigarette Man had moved to start this mess. But we did agree with him that Cigarette Man did not move when the shotguns were pointed right at him.

And so that dark night, the young St. Robert officer became a legend on the night shift. A crime fighting demon, if you will. Later in his long career, Patrolman Ron Long, of the St. Robert Police department, went on to become an undercover narc in the state of Texas. He moved back to Missouri and, as I left the elected office of Sheriff of Pulaski County at midnight on 12-31-2012, Sheriff Ron Long took over the reins of the office at one minute after midnight. He even went so far as to write a couple of books thus making Ron and me most likely the only two Missouri Sheriff's in history to accomplish that feat. Especially from the same county.

Postscript; Serious words for once. I greatly respect Ron Long and his accomplishments in the field of Law Enforcement so let's be clear that I consulted with him prior to writing this story and I have his permission to tell all. Also, in all fairness, there was this heating air duct just a few inches from the Cigarette Man that was blowing air toward the cardboard figure and it is possible that Cigarette Man may have moved. But that simple fact lessens the impact of an otherwise real good story.

38 THE PIMP'S REVENGE

As previously mentioned in this book, most evenings the Troopers on duty would get together and pick out one house of ill repute to go visit. This was a solid crime-fighting technique and kept us in the know on bad guys in our immediate area. Occasionally, when we did this, weird things happened. This story is just such a case.

On this particular rainy evening, we had chosen a house of ill repute located near the Missouri 28/ I-44 overpass. There were three of us Troopers that night with the most senior man leading the way. As the junior Trooper, I was at the rear of the convoy. As we pulled into the parking lot of the house of ill repute, the lead Trooper suddenly started yelling, "Shots fired, shots fired!"

The three of us bailed out, guns drawn, ready for combat. The first thing we saw was the head pimp of the establishment and several of his girls standing on the front porch staring out across the muddy parking lot and laughing their butts off. This was not exactly the scene that had just flashed in front of our eyes, but the pimp had a . 45 in his hand. We quickly relieved him of his toy and he continued laughing.

The initial impression was this was not a dangerous shots fired situation. Since we were in contact with the pimp, he immediately gave us the story of what had happened. It seems that a male patron of the establishment had paid his money and was in the small room with the lady in question ready for action. He was feeling frisky and was ready for heavy "action." However the lady was not feeling very frisky and was basically just lying there very stoic and unmoving. The patron decided that he needed his money's worth and definitely needed more action. So the patron proceeded to wrap his hands around her neck, depriving her of oxygen and this produced a great deal of physical effort on her part. Very frisky.

All was going well for him, not so well for the lady, when the head pimp arrived on the scene and stuck the barrel of the .45 caliber pistol in the patron's ear and asked him what the hell was he doing? The buck naked guy dismounted at full speed and fled into the parking lot.

He was last seen running across the muddy parking lot in the rain at full speed. Things went downhill as the laughing pimp and ladies watched him run. The pimp decided to fire off a couple of rounds skyward. The naked man increased his running speed considerably. And with perfect timing, enter the Troopers onto the scene. At this point, the senior Trooper who had led us into the parking lot said, "Hey wait a second, I saw that naked guy running across the parking lot." This confirmed the pimp's story and pretty much deflated a shots fired scene.

The other senior Trooper went after the guy in the rain and pretty soon came driving back with a very wet, muddy, naked guy in the backseat of his car, wrapped up in the blanket that we all carried in the trunk of our vehicle. We arranged for the patron to retrieve his clothing and, after he got dressed, we escorted him to his car and then escorted him off the premises. And the shots fired situation came to a very peaceful end.

Postscript: Try going from a "shots fired" danger call, to sixty seconds later standing in the rain, in a muddy parking lot, with a pimp and several working girls and everybody, including the boys in blue, laughing their cans off. It was an emotional roller coaster for sure. I forgot to mention the guy was embarrassed to say the least. St. Robert of this era was absolutely never boring.

39 JB'S LAST GOOD DEED

As I have said several times in this book, when you start a work shift with the Highway Patrol, you never quite know what you're going to get into before the day is over. As I neared the end of my thirty-two year career, with an anticipated retirement date of July 1, 2001, I was kind of surprised to receive a thank you letter from a citizen for something I had done on the highway.

The letter was brought to my attention on June 14, 2001. The letter was written about a good deed that I done on June 3, 2001. I assisted a sick motorist roadside and the young lad had not been able to get my name. His mother had sent a message to the General Headquarters of the Missouri State Highway Patrol in Jefferson City about the incident and they referred it back to Troop I.

When they went looking at Troop I in the radio log, to try and discover who the officer was that the young lad was talking about, they found an entry that clearly said it was me and on that radio log sheet that was copied and included as part of the packet with the letter somebody had penciled in the words, "JB's last good deed." And I am going to confess that simple sentence touched me deeply.

So here is the story of JB's last good deed.

On June 3, 2001, during routine patrol, I had just driven east to the Route J overpass, which is just barely inside Phelps County and was turning around to go back west into Pulaski County. As I got to the end of the entrance ramp to I-44, I saw motorist parked on the shoulder and as I parked my vehicle behind his, I watched the motorist throw up on the right away in front of his car. And that action explained immediately why he was stopped.

When I went up to talk to the young lad, who was standing there, he told me that he felt sick to his stomach and just couldn't help throwing up and that everything was okay. He said he was headed for Tulsa, Oklahoma. As we stood there talking for a moment or two, I happened to glance down at the pool of vomit at my feet and immediately saw fresh red blood in the vomit along with black bricks of coagulated blood that was clearly several days old. A lot of red blood. Immediate medical diagnosis, severe bleeding ulcer, surgery probably in his immediate future.

I told the young lad this and he basically was indifferent. He said that he was going to Tulsa and he just would continue on and check in with the doctor there. I told him he would not make Tulsa with this condition and urged him to turn around go back to his residence in Rolla, which he did not want to do.

After several minutes, I told him, "Look, if you continue west, you're going to pass out and run off the road or you're going to pull over and pass out and, when you do, I'm loading you in an ambulance and sending you to the hospital. So you have a choice do that or turn around and go back home."

He finally agreed to go back home. I got him turned around and headed back east toward Rolla. I stayed conspicuously behind him for quite some distance into Phelps County until I was sure that he was going to go home.

And now to finish the story, I would like to quote from the letter that his mother sent to the Highway Patrol and it reads as follows, "On June 3 somewhere around two or 3 o'clock in the afternoon, our son, (name redacted) left to return to Tulsa, Oklahoma. About 10 miles out of Rolla he pulled off I-44 because he was sick. One of your Trooper's stopped to help and wanted to take him to the hospital. Adam refused of course (because that's what men do), but the officer convinced him he was too sick to go on (actually he made a dead accurate diagnosis on the spot), got him to the other lane and escorted him back to town to make sure he got to our house safely. Just minutes after Adam arrived he passed out and we took him to the ER where they found he had a severely bleeding ulcer and had lost half of his blood volume! (No mom, I'm fine. It's just something I ate.) He was operated on to stop the bleeding and now he is doing fine."

"Adam was too sick to see the officer's name but he said he was a "big Highway Patrol looking guy with a crew cut". If you can identify the trooper from the above time and location would you please tell him how very grateful we all are for his help. I don't even want to think about what might've happened if a "big Highway Patrol looking guy" hadn't convinced Adam that he was sicker than he wanted to admit. Another half hour or so on the road might have been disastrous." Case closed.

ABOUT THE AUTHOR

J.B. King is a former two-term sheriff of Pulaski County and author. Among his published work includes this book as well as "Tilly Treasure" and "Justice," not to mention a plethora of Sheriff's Views and columns written for the local newspaper, the Waynesville Daily Guide. He's a Civil War enthusiast, story teller, and history buff. He has several other books in the planning and research phases, so readers can expect more from him in the genre of true crime and history. He resides in Pulaski County with his lovely wife, Cheryl, their son, Taylor, and their giant puppy Chloe.